BECOMING
H.E.R.O.I.C.

Shane McGraw

BECOMING H.E.R.O.I.C.
How to Protect Your Family, Finances, and Future.

Copyright © 2017 by Shane McGraw. All rights reserved.

Published by:
Shane McGraw Team
Silverdale, WA
(360) 519-7567
www.shanemcgrawteam.com

All Rights Reserved. No part of this book may be used or reproduced in
any manner whatsoever without the expressed written permission of the
author. Address all inquiries to:

Shane McGraw
Telephone: 360-519-7567
Email: mcgrawshane@gmail.com
www.shanemcgrawteam.com

ISBN - 13: 978-1978031395

ISBN - 10: 1978031394

Editor: Tyler Tichelaar
Cover Designer: Rebekah E. Ahlsten
Interior Book Layout: Rebekah E. Ahlsten

Every attempt has been made to properly source all quotes.

Printed in the United States of America

This book is dedicated to my wife and family. And to the military men and women who graciously and heroically devote their lives to the service of our freedom and liberties.

CONTENTS

	Acknowledgments	i
	Introduction	3
1	Have Purpose	27
2	Entrepreneur Mindset	67
3	Relationships	89
4	Overall Health	133
5	Incentive Hunter	147
6	Courage and Commitment	163
7	A Final Note	177
8	Resources	181

ACKNOWLEDGMENTS

Jim Rohn, Og Mandingo, Dale Carnegie, Louse Thaxton, General Tommy Franks, Gary Vaynerchuk, and Darren Hardy.

INTRODUCTION

My story is a depiction of the American dream. I came from nothing—raised in the home of an abusive, mean, drug-addicted father. Through determination and grit, I now own multiple businesses and live a wonderful and happy life with my wife and family. Given my upbringing, I never could have imagined my life would be this full. Everything in my world conditioned me for a life of failure and pain. However, I was able to change the course of my trajectory through learned skills, intentional choices, and a forward-thinking mindset. Now it is my fervent desire to impart these tools to everyone who desires to be the hero of their own story. *Becoming H.E.R.O.I.C.* is an honest examination of the ups and downs that led me to a thriving life. It is designed to be an asset and tool as you begin *your* journey toward a healthier and more successful future!

MISSION: H.E.R.O.I.C

One of my personal and professional goals is to be a hero for the heroes that protect our freedoms through daily sacrifice and service. The purpose of the H.E.R.O.I.C. model is to break life into six manageable and practical categories. The primary objective is to move from a "Drifting" mindset to a "Directed" mindset in each one of these groupings.

- **H** – Have Purpose
- **E** – Entrepreneur Mindset
- **R** – Relationships
- **O** – Overall Health
- **I** – Incentive Hunter
- **C** – Courage and Commitment

DEVELOP YOUR ROADMAP

A map is a visual representation of roads used for travel and navigation. It is essential when traveling to someplace new or unfamiliar.

It contains relevant data and allows you to develop a plan of action. In the same way, a clear plan for how to implement the H.E.R.O.I.C. steps is crucial for consistency and lasting change. This book will provide the instruments for effective change. However, tools sitting on a workbench are worthless. They need to be *used* to yield results!

Many heroes find it useful to begin every day getting into the right mindset, whether that be ten minutes of journaling or reflecting on the attributes of a hero. Perhaps it is reviewing personal progress or reexamining future goals. Getting pumped up is essential! This includes anything

that provides you with the motivation to live into your heroic nature! Another system that many find useful is to spend each day of the week with the corresponding H.E.R.O.I.C. category. For instance (Mondays = H, Tuesday = E... and so on. Sunday is dedicated to reflection). Regardless of the specific details of your roadmap, be sure that you are actively implementing this system every day!

Within each of these sections there will be the following checkpoints:

1. **A Roadmap** – A roadmap is presented for each category in the H.E.R.O.I.C. model. This offers a clear understanding of the purpose and goals of each section. Use it as a personal assessment tool to honestly examine where you are in the journey. It will also allow you to revisit areas of weakness or struggle to tackle hang-ups and struggles. The more times you look at a map, the more familiar you become with the terrain, pitfalls, and shortcuts. Revisit these roadmaps as often as you need to ensure you are winning in all areas of the H.E.R.O.I.C. life.

2. **Personal Stories and Lessons** – Some people can learn from the pain and mistakes of

others; while others need to hit every bump in the road with their head to know that it hurts. These accounts (mostly personal – although I have been permitted to share some stories from other people in my life) are meant to present an honest evaluation of what works and what is a waste of time. While I freely give my tips for success, it is equally important that I openly recount my failures and shortcomings. Please learn from the bumps I have acquired so that you can spare your head on the highway of life!

3. **Personal Reflection Questions** – This checkpoint is meant to be enjoyable and help you genuinely reflect. This is the opportunity to take a good look at your current status and set goals accordingly.

4. **Act NOW!** – The best dieting advice I ever heard: Do not wait until Monday to start your diet! Start now! These exercises are intended to be done immediately. Literally, throw this book down and put muscles to thoughts! Scientists have proven that the more ways you can physically engage with the material you are trying to learn, the more likely it will directly impact your life. If you are aiming for

real H.E.R.O.I.C. change, put boots to thoughts and act NOW! These activities are also an excellent place for accountability and teamwork!

5. **Homework** – This section is pretty self-explanatory. But this is not the life-sucking school mumbo-jumbo. This is fun, life-giving stuff that helps you be a better, happier, healthier, and wealthier person! If you are part of an H.E.R.O.I.C. team, the Act NOW and homework sections will particularly benefit you and your fellow heroes while you journey together!

6. **Find a Mentor** – *Becoming H.E.R.O.I.C* will serve as your primary mentor throughout your heroic journey. However, the more people that invest in your life, the more impactful and lasting the results. As such, this section of will focus on mentorship attributes to seek out in the people that surround you. They can be your co-workers, superiors, friends, family or wise people that speak truth into your life and have a sincere desire to invest in your success. In life, there is always someone who will have "bigger pile" than you. Whether it be in relationships, work, life skills, parenting or

general knowledge. Someone will always be smarter or more experienced. The goal is to find people with "bigger piles" and invite them to share their knowledge and expertise with you!

7. **Get Connected** – The H.E.R.O.I.C. movement will not be accomplished in isolation! Connecting with others is a fundamental part of H.E.R.O.I.C. success and sustainability. Join the *Becoming H.E.R.O.I.C.* community on social media for additional motivation, support and creative ideas for practical implementation of the H.E.R.O.I.C. model. The online *Becoming H.E.R.O.I.C.* also provides further questions for assessment and actions steps to track your progress. As a result, this book stays relevant whether it is your first day in the military, your last day on the job or it finds you long past the time that you served your country. I look forward to taking this journey together! We are about to embark on an incredible and heroic journey toward success. It will be tough, it will be dirty, and it will require blood, sweat, and tears. However, to the victor goes the spoils!

BE THE HERO OF YOUR OWN STORY

Let me start off by saying, I love the military! Men and women who lay down their lives every day to protect the freedoms of this great nation are real heroes. If you are in the military, then I wrote this book with exceptional consideration for you. In the face of danger, you combat adversity through impressive feats of ingenuity, bravery, and strength. Furthermore, you sacrifice your concerns for a greater good and a higher purpose. You deserve recognition and praise for your sacrifice and your devotion. Thank you!

> **THIS BOOK GIVES YOU THE TOOLS TO BE THE HERO OF YOUR OWN STORY!**

There is no denying that our military service members are the true heroes. Unfortunately, for many, they are not living as the heroes of their own stories and lives. Military personnel tends to be one of the most indebted groups of people in our country. They also have one of the highest divorce rates and suicide rates. Typically they tend to struggle in areas of family, friends, and money. The pressures and challenges that "come with the job" take a toll on their relationships, health, and overall well-being. The military is very good at creating soldiers, yet this is often at the expense of the soldier's personal life. The H.E.R.O.I.C. model is designed to help you turn the tide and set you up for success. This book was written to let you know that I am one of you. I love the military. I am here for you, and I want to use every tool in my belt to ensure you have a bright and prosperous future. You are already a hero to everyone else; now is the time to be a hero in your own story!

Many of the principles in this book are derived from personal accounts of my time in service. Primarily intended to help those in the military, these tactics apply to anyone. The average age of our military is 18-25 years. From a human development perspective, a majority of our military force is at the age where adolescence is coming to an end, and they are determining the type of people they want to be for the rest of their lives. Often, major life decisions occur during this phase—what to do for a career, whether to get married or not and the establishment of habits that will determine the trajectory of life.

THIS IS YOUR SUCCESS PLAYBOOK

What would happen if you were handed a Success Playbook on the first day of your military career—be it active duty enlisted, officer, reservist, or some other type of service? This military-cheat-sheet gives you all the practical tools to Be H.E.R.O.I.C. and have great success in your personal and professional goals.

This book unpacks the six major areas of the H.E.R.O.I.C. life with the mindset of The Compound Impact. Small, consistent investments of time and energy in six critical areas of life will award you with long-lasting results! Imagine a bank account that you deposit into every day. Some days, a lot of money goes into the account; some days only a little. But you always add *something*. That account will grow and grow. Now if you invested that same growing amount into meaningful accounts that accumulated positive interest, you would be wealthy beyond belief! The same concept works in reverse. For example, credit card companies make their fortunes by taking a small withdrawal and adding interest so you charge more over time and it takes longer to pay off.

What if you spent each day making small deposits into six major areas of your H.E.R.O.I.C. life? This book is meant to be a toolkit to ensure you are building a wealthy living and investing in tomorrow rather than going into metaphoric, or literal, debt and robbing your future happiness. Each area of focus has checkpoints that, if practiced daily, will garner success and incredible returns over the long haul. Good decisions give way to more good decisions. In the same way, bad decisions lead to worse decisions and, ultimately, to catastrophic ones. Allow the compound impact to work for you, not against you!

Living life with the H.E.R.O.I.C. mindset means that you recognize the opportunity and the blessings that your service is to our country and yourself. The H.E.R.O.I.C. life is a chance to learn, grow, and invest in now and the future by being present and strategic with each moment. With the proven H.E.R.O.I.C. tools, tactics, mindsets, and resources you will be equipped to:
- Maximize time in service through personal and professional investments.
- Create the building blocks to be highly successful after your time in service.

This book will provide the toolkit to help optimize your time now, so you will be prepared to launch into the next chapter of your life – be it retirement, a second career, or even starting your own business. The methods in this book have proven to be successful regardless of past circumstances, financial status, past regrets, or future hopes. If you genuinely take these principles to heart, you will see immediate personal, physical, professional, and psychological improvements. This system is designed to meet you where you are and get you to where you want to go!

Not many of us are great leaders, but many of us are good leaders with the potential for greatness. Greatness is developed, not born. *Becoming H.E.R.O.I.C.* is designed to serve as a guide to educate, empower, and equip you with the tools necessary not to squander your personal and professional gifts. However, this process will not be a walk in the park. It will require pure grit, determination, the right mindset and personal fortitude. Do you have what it takes?

THE RIGHT MINDSET

One of the most valuable lessons in life is the discovery that everything comes down to mental state and stamina. Having the right mindset has the power to change

> **BE PROACTIVE IN YOUR THINKING, NOT REACTIVE IN YOUR RESPONSES!**

your attitude, your relationships, and your entire reality. Early in life, you likely realized that life is 10 percent about what happens to you and 90 percent about how you respond. Typically you cannot change *what happens* in life. Many people try and often fail, to control every component of their reality. They drive themselves (and everyone else) crazy trying to micromanage their environments and the people around them to make life "go their way." Even if that were possible (and it is not!), that math sucks. You are only winning 10 percent of the game!

Mental toughness is frequently used to describe positive attributes that help a person cope with stressful situations. It is a measure of individual resilience and confidence that may predict success in sports, education, and the workplace. It allows a person to become better able to cope with difficult or competitive situations and emerge without losing confidence. Mental toughness gives you the tenacity to learn from your mistakes without allowing failures to become devastating blows. Resilience and fortitude also provide the strength to keep emotions in check when circumstances are overwhelming, and you need to be strong. It is the voice in the back of your head that tells you to keep going, keep pushing, and keep trying, even when circumstances are rough.

Having mental toughness is the key to winning at life (or at least scoring a 90 percent)! Regardless of the circumstance (best day ever, excellent, fair, mediocre, sucky, or the worst day imaginable), there is always a decision to make: How am I going to *respond* to what just happened to me? It is imperative that you do not have a reactionary approach to life and circumstances. That will not produce the mental strength necessary to live an H.E.R.O.I.C. life.

What if you dedicated your time to become the best version of yourself? What would it look like if you stayed mission-focused with your time and made every day count? The equation is simple:

1 Part Attitude + 2 Parts Effort = Success

Having the right mindset will make certain that you have the right attitude. The right attitude will ensure that you start the day with the correct approach. The effort will guarantee that your daily actions follow suit. Grit and mental fortitude will align your daily actions with your desired objective. As a result, you will become more skilled, smarter, healthier, and be set up to achieve your goals in life and next adventure!

ONE BITE AT A TIME!

Changing habits and behaviors can be a daunting task. How does one possibly modify attitudes and actions that have likely been practiced and implemented for years, perhaps decades? Well, how do you eat an elephant? The answer: one bite at a time. *Starting* each day with the correct attitude and then being intentional about making good choices *throughout* the day is the key to lasting change. It will NOT be easy. Sometimes, it will not be fun. And it will take everything you have and then more! Are you ready to choose to have the right mindset? Are you willing to make daily decisions to transform yourself into your full H.E.R.O.I.C. potential?

DRIFTING, DRIVEN, DIRECTED

If you are breathing, you likely fall in one of these three categories: drifting, driven or directed.

Drifting

Those drifting through life are like a cork or bobbers in the water. There is no clear idea of purpose or function on this earth. People who are Drifting tend to scramble around looking for various ways to cope with life or survive it. It is a reactionary mindset. As a result, they are easily influenced by peers to participate in "fun" activities that only lead to bad decisions or painful events. These reactions typically include illicit drugs, sex, alcohol, partying, or other illegal activities. This season is somewhat appropriate in youth, however, if one gets stuck in the drifting phase, it is incredibly challenging to be successful or healthy in the long-term.

Driven

This mindset comes from a period of discontentment and the realization that drifting through life will lead nowhere. As a result, this is usually a time of high motivation and self-promotion. These two qualities are a double-edged sword. Having a Driven mindset will often propel you toward purpose and goals. Unfortunately, this mentality is typically all about self-focused ambition. Like the driver of any vehicle or boat, they will power towards their destination despite bad weather, darkness, or obstacles. Yes, they will get there, but how many things did they run over in the process and how enjoyable was the ride for their fellow passengers? Even the word Driven has "I" near the core. Someone at this stage is typically focused on themselves and what they can get regardless of the cost of others. This period tends to lead to productivity and success. However, because it is rooted in selfish desire and intention, there tends to be a lot of hurt, isolation, loneliness, compromise, and pain along the way.

Directed

To help illustrate this, picture a huge sailing ship, like the USS Constitution. The USS

Constitution was the first ship commissioned by the U.S. Navy. In 1797 this massive, three-mast boat had a crew of 450, 55 Marines and 30 boys. Equipped with the right assets, armory, and expertise, this ship became a force of the ocean and the Naval Fleet. It was beautiful, powerful, and fast. It became a national symbol of the dedication, courage, and achievement of American fighting men and ships. Throughout her entire service life, she was never boarded by hostile forces and is still in commission over 220 years later!

Like this mighty ship, the Directed life is one that utilizes the multiple resources available (wind, currents, manual labor) to accomplish mighty missions. There is a clear understanding that personal ownership and responsibility are not negotiable. A person living a Directed life knows that they must first work on themselves before they can lead or influence others – they fill their cup to ensure that they can pour into others. Someone living the Directed life also has the wisdom to use team members to their fullest potential. When one member of the team succeeds, everyone celebrates; when one fails everyone rallies to support.

Becoming H.E.R.O.I.C.

Drifting

- Life Goal: WTF
- No clear vision or purpose
- "Just along for the ride."
- Success and failure is largely determined by other people

Driven

Life Goal: I am going to "Get Mine"!
Purpose: to gain personal success and establish self-worth.
Self-focused
Master of Own Destiny
Success and failure is largely determined by self-motivation and determination.

Directed

- Life Goal: I am going to leave a legacy and help others win!
- Purpose: to help others through solid relationships and personal investment.
- Confident and self-assured leader of many.
- Success and failure is the product of group success and effort.
- It is as if you are doing things for a greater purpose.

WARNING! THIS BOOK IS NOT FOR WIMPS!

People in the military are fighters, defenders, warriors, and patriots. We are persevering, hard-working, and gritty. We do not stop—no matter what. We do not turn back—no matter how hard things get. No mountain is insurmountable. No task is too great. To every soldier, sailor, marine, and airman who is worthy of the call, if the mission is to live a full and fruitful life, perseverance is the battle cry.

Now is the time that we *stop* floundering and wasting time with inferior marriages, bad finances, and diminishing health. We need to be prepared to face the challenges of life and learn how to thrive! There are decisions you will make this very moment that will affect the type of person you are and the type of lifestyle you will have tomorrow. To face life with

> **WE NEED TO BE PREPARED TO FACE THE CHALLENGES OF LIFE AND LEARN HOW TO THRIVE!**

intentionality takes courage and resolve. Below are several elements that are necessary to develop the grit and determination the H.E.R.O.I.C. model requires:

- **Pick Your Pain:** There are two different types of pain in life: the pain of staying the same or the pain of changing. Change in behavior comes when the fear of changing outweighs the pain of staying the same.

- **Prepare for Challenges:** Change is hard. Life and business are filled with everyday demands, the occasional crisis, and unexpected twists. Have the fortitude to withstand the professional and personal hardships you will inevitably be facing.

- **Strength under Stress:** Maintain resilience in the face of adverse pressures by developing your capacity to deal with stressful situations.

- **Tenacity:** It comes down to just three words: Never give up!

- **Readiness for Change:** Flexibility and adaptability are among the most important traits you can develop.

- **Endurance in the Face of Failure:** View failure as an opportunity to grow and improve, not a reason to give up. Be willing to keep trying until you get it right.

Doing more than what is expected is the secret sauce to the H.E.R.O.I.C. life. This book and this lifestyle are not intended for half-hearted people. If you do not have what it takes to jump on the grenade for someone else (even if, metaphorically, that is you)—stop reading! The H.E.R.O.I.C. model is for the people who live up to that name. They have a fire in their bellies and a burning passion in their hearts. If this sounds like you, join the countless others who choose to live for each moment and work hard to support our fellow heroes in their efforts. Fair warning: wusses are *not* welcome!

> JOIN THE COUNTLESS OTHERS WHO CHOOSE TO LIVE FOR EACH MOMENT AND WORK HARD TO SUPPORT OUR FELLOW HEROES.

Are you ready to start this journey towards becoming H.E.R.O.I.C.? Good. Then let's begin!

My goal is to provide the tools to equip you to become the hero of your own story! This is your guide, a playbook if you will. The H.E.R.O.I.C. model offers the building blocks for the rest of your life. Irreducible minimums that lay the foundation to support you now and in the future. What if at the end of your service (for those of you not in the military, what if at the end of the next five years) you could confidently check six boxes that would ensure you have been wise and set the stage for a full, successful life. I am so excited for the opportunity to embark on this H.E.R.O.I.C. journey together!

SHOW ME HOW TO TAKE WHO I AM, WHO I WANT TO BE, AND WHAT I CAN DO, AND USE IT FOR A PURPOSE GREATER THAN MYSELF.

– MARTIN LUTHER KING JR.

H.E.R.O.I.C.

CHAPTER ONE:

HAVE PURPOSE

DRIFTING:
No purpose in life/
Not intentional about life.

DRIVEN:
My purpose meets my needs and contributes to my success.

DIRECTED:
My purpose benefits both myself and others.

PURPOSE OUT OF CHAOS

My dad was a drug addict. Drugs came into the picture and caused tremendous violence in my family. As the oldest child, my mom pulled me aside and said, *"If this happens, I want you to save your brother and sister."* It did not take long for it to happen... again. My dad started beating my mom, and I was forced to leave her behind. I crawled out of a window with my brother and sister. We went to a nearby park bench and waited for the chaos to stop before we returned home. While sitting on that bench, I had a pivotal moment. I was utterly helpless. I was old enough to be aware of all that was happening, but I was not in a position to do anything about it. My mom, my only safety net, was helpless and unable to help me. My dad was "the crazy guy." He was responsible for the madness of my childhood. However, like all children, I wanted his love, acceptance, and guidance. He knew that and used it as a weapon to tear me down and wound me. This was the cycle of my youth. Sitting on that park bench, all those feelings hurt, pain, anguish, and abandonment started to come to the surface. Suddenly, a surreal peace came over me. Decades later, I still remember how I physically felt in that instant. Then a thought came to me. It was like a train approaching from a distance. It started small and quickly came into focus, horns blazing. I was overcome with a reassuring thought: *My legacy will not be this. I will create a new legacy.*

No matter what happened in my life following that day, I could always hold on to that hope. I carried it around like a badge of honor. At times it was a source of pride. I would think *Oh you wait. I will be better than that!* I still had some growing to do but it was a lifeline – it became the start of my purpose. What has served as your park bench moment?

Everyone has a purpose in life. However, if you do not honestly believe that, you will spend a majority of your time Drifting through life. The better part of my youth and early twenties, I was a drifter. My experience was not about where I wanted to go; it was how to survive the Hell that was my reality. I lived in that abusive environment until I was seventeen. At that time I stood up to my stepfather and won. Consequently, I was kicked out of the house. I spent the next two years as a homeless, couch-crasher. Eventually, I spent some time in my grandparents' home. My Grandfather all but demanded I join the military – I had few options and fewer prospects. I enlisted through the Delayed Entry Program, finished high school, and was shipped off to Basic Training.

Unfortunately, a good portion of my early military career continued this prolonged state of Drifting. On the first day of Basic Training, I realized that being an emotional and stubborn man was going to be very bad if I wanted to have a successful career. Although my mind knew that, I did not easily give up the coping mechanisms from childhood. The stubborn side of my personality, allowed me to survive my father's house – so it took some time for that to be rooted out. While I did have successes in the military (opportunities to travel, ability to learn, experience different cultures), I made my fair share of mistakes (too many women, too much drinking, breaking a man's jaw, fighting, and worse of all – not being intentional). There are many more stories, but for now, it is sufficient to say that if I had been deliberate about figuring out my purpose then (even if it changed), it would have spared me a lot of needless grief and heartache.

WHAT IS YOUR PURPOSE?

Every well-written paper has a thesis. Every successful military mission has a primary target and objective. Every excellent business deal has an intended outcome. This is the purpose. *What are you living for?* This is where the hero must start. Why? Because how we honestly define our purpose will determine:

> …The decisions we make.
>
> …Our financial, health and personal priorities.
>
> …How we spend our time and resources.
>
> …The way we treat others.
>
> …Ultimately, the type of person we turn out to be.

A *Drifting* Higher Purpose: A Drifting person does not consider higher purpose. Little or no thought is given to anything beyond the here and now. Most decisions are made based on what feels right at the moment. Like the adage says, "If you do not stand for something, you will fall for anything."

A *Driven* Higher Purpose: A Driven person has objectives but only a little perspective. For instance, someone might decide to make their purpose in life to become rich. As a result, money becomes the focus of all their decisions and actions. The almighty dollar will drive them. They spend a majority of their time thinking about how to make money and then a ton of time pursuing wealth. People and time become commodities. It is likely that they will make sacrifices in relationships if those people interfere with making money. Also, if money is the priority, someone is less likely to share or be generous with their time or their possessions.

A *Directed* Higher Purpose: A Directed hero is enthusiastic about leaving a legacy. As a result, the focus shifts from themselves to a passion. This will manifest as a desire to work hard to pursue a goal. Objectives are met with the perspective of serving others. They will network with other passionate individuals. Overall, people will be treated with care and respect because relationships are central to leaving a legacy.

Culturally and instinctually we are programmed to take before we give. We need to look out for #1 and make as much as we can from people and situations. Many mistakenly believe this is the path to success. How can I get the most in life without having to give anything?

Plenty of people perpetuate this notion of a higher good. I am not talking about *the* higher good. I am talking about *your* higher good. The H.E.R.O.I.C. life has purpose and meaning. Most importantly, real heroes are NOT at the center of their purpose. If you want all the things in your world, and want to make a difference, you cannot perpetuate the notion *it is all about me*. Nobody cares! Instead, you must propagate others first. It just so happens that when you live with this heroic perspective, you often get what you want. However, the order does matter. Anyone who has built their success on the backs of others without respect for this process has either lost it or not been fulfilled by it. Therefore if you want to achieve your objectives in life, it is vital to have Purpose and ensure it is more significant than a single individual!

PRACTICAL TIPS FOR DEFINING YOUR PURPOSE

1. **Must be greater than self.**
   - Who or what do you look to when you reach the end of yourself?
     - This provides motivation when things get tough.
     - This also gives hope during seasons of failures or obstacles.
2. **Must be phrased in a positive tone.**
   - "I will create a new legacy" vs. "I will not suck like you."
     - This creates personal ownership rather than passing blame.
     - A positive outlook makes goals more achievable and objectives more clear.
3. **Must consider the "End Game."**
   - Write your eulogy. Sounds morbid, but it helps to focus your priorities.
     - What will people say about you when you are gone?
   - Helps align where to spend time, money, and resources.
   - If actions do not line up with goals, what needs to change?

Personal Reflection Questions:

In an effort to be intentional and purposeful in life, spend approximately 10 or 15 minutes considering the following questions:

1. What makes you smile? (Activities, people, events, hobbies, projects, etc.)
2. What are your favorite things to do in the past? What about now?
3. What causes you to lose track of time?
4. What makes you feel great about yourself?
5. Who inspires you most? (Anyone you know or do not. Family, friends, authors, artists, leaders, etc.) Which qualities encourage you, in each person?
6. What are you naturally good at? (Skills, abilities, gifts, etc.)
7. People typically ask for your help doing...
8. If you had to teach something, what would you teach?
9. What would you regret not fully doing, being or having in your life?
10. You are now 90 years old. Looking back at your life and all your achievements and relationships; what matters to you most? List them out.

11. What are your deepest values? Please select 3-5, and put in order most important to you:

Adventure	Friendship	Passion
Beauty	Giving	Performance
Being the best	Health	Personal Growth
Challenge	Honesty	Play
Comfort	Independence	Productivity
Courage	Inner peace	Relationship
Creativity	Intelligence	Reliability
Curiosity	Intimacy	Respect
Education	Joy	Security
Empowerment	Leadership	Spirituality
Environment	Learning	Success
Family	Love	Time freedom
Fiscal freedom	Motivation	Variety

12. What were some challenges or hardships you have overcome or are in the process of overcoming? How did you do it?
13. What causes do you firmly believe in? Connect with?
14. If you could get a message across to a large group of people. Who would those people be? What would your message be?
15. Given your talents, passions, and values. How could you use these resources to serve, help, and contribute?

Act NOW!

<u>Time Limit</u>: 1 Hour

<u>Mission</u>:

- Find three (3) people.
    - These people may fit any of the following criteria: your spouse, family members, friends, people that you trust, people you work with, or conveniently placed strangers!
- Tell them your goal! Something like, "Today I have decided that I am going to be intentional about my future!" or "Over the next few weeks/months I am going to work on becoming a better version of me!"
    - If you do not have people around:
        - Call, send text messages or emails, or write a letter.
- Ask them to hold you accountable!
    - Set up an Accountability Schedule
    - For example, "In a couple of weeks will you please ask me about it?" or "Let's check-in in a couple of days and report what we have learned!"

Homework:

1. Write your own Eulogy.
    a. What do you want people to say about you?
    b. What do you want to be remembered for?
2. Write your Life's Mission Statement.
    a. Keep in mind that this is bound to change eventually. However, what is your Mission Statement Today?

Find A Mentor:

1. Who is the most driven, motivated, focused, and grittiest person you know?
    a. Why they do the things they do?
    b. What keeps them motivated and striving for success?

Get Connected:

- Post Your Purpose! Log onto our Facebook page and tell us your purpose!
- Get a picture of your mentors! #MYHEROICMENTOR

LOVING PROFITABLE RELATIONSHIPS

I have never met one person that has said any of the following:

Man, I want to suck at my job today.

I try to be a terrible husband or father.

My goal is to be a horrible friend.

I hope that I make bad decisions with money and struggle financially.

However, our actions speak louder than our words. For example, some men live in the reality of a being a terrible husband and father because they put their own needs before the needs of their family. Loving Profitable Relationships (LPR) bridges the gap between doing the right things and having the right purpose. When these two elements come together, life

> **LPR BRIDGES THE GAP BETWEEN DOING THE RIGHT THINGS AND HAVING THE RIGHT PURPOSE.**

becomes incredibly rich and rewarding. To understand how to do this, let us take a look at the individual components of Loving Profitable Relationships and how these elements fit into living the H.E.R.O.I.C. life.

Loving

Love is measured so uniquely. I *love* my dog. I *love* my wife. I *love* my parents. I *love* this steak. And all these *loves* are different. In the English language, love may be used to describe a variety of things and experiences. As a result, the word love does not carry the same weight it does in other languages that have different "love" words for passionate, brotherly, sexual, casual, satisfying or unquenchable affection. Unfortunately, because of this, the word and the concept of *love* has become muddled. In the purest form of love, some things are not negotiable: mutual trust, selflessness, and vulnerability. For my wife and me to fully love one another, we must both be actively making the needs of the other person a priority. The result is two full independent people choosing to be vulnerable and selfless. The result is a shared trust. Only then do we as a couple have the ability to connect to something bigger and deeper than either one of us (i.e. religion, dreams, talents, hopes, etc).

If you understand love, then money does not matter. Love leads to generosity and generosity leads to clarity on cash. Wealth is not about how much money you make but how can you use that money to enrich the lives of other people. It just so happens that the more you influence and affect people, the more they will want to bless you in return. This typically means that you make more money as a result!

Profitable

Similarly, many people misunderstand the concept of profitable. Many believe that it has to do with money or the exchange of money. In actuality, it has little, if anything, to do with money. Rather, it is a value proposition between two people which leaves both parties *more complete together* than *individually*. In essence, this is the "sum is greater than the individual parts" philosophy. Profit is like love – fluid and dynamic. Think about people or friends that are continually uplifting and encouraging. They make you feel special and important. Even though there is no monetary exchange; there is an exchange of value. They are enjoyable and make you want to be a better person. That is profitable. The exciting thing is that money almost always follows profit.

Relationships

Relationships are beyond dynamic and complex. As such, an entire chapter will be dedicated to discussing how to have success in various types of relationships. However, the purpose of relationships and the foundation of relationships must be included in the *WHY* of everything that you do. To be personally or professionally successful, an intentional decision must be made about relationships and their function in daily life.

- Do you want to have friends?
- Do you want others to like you?
- Do you want to impact others positively?
- Do you want to be able to share your deepest secrets with someone and know they will love you and stick by your side?
- Do you want to be able to share the rewards of your success with those you love?

If you answer *yes* to most of these questions, then successful and healthy relationships are essential in your life. Fortunately, by replying yes to these questions, we have also established that you are not a robot! Humans were designed to be in healthy and mutually beneficial relationships. When all goes according to plan, both parties benefit and life is pleasurable, peaceful and full. Unfortunately, when things do not go well, relationships are the source of great pain and heartache. This book will give you the tools for happy and satisfied relationships. However, before any skills may be implemented, you must decide if healthy and beneficial relationships are a priority and worth the effort that is required.

When the desire and determination to have genuine relationships that are loving and profitable become the focus and purpose of your life, all other elements of the H.E.R.O.I.C. life come into focus. LPR galvanizes all the components of the H.E.R.O.I.C. life through a higher purpose and calling. Loving Profitable Relationships provides the framework and the motivation for successful business dealings, beneficial relationships, and a positive lifestyle.

Personal Reflection Questions:

1. Please list the Name and Relationship of the seven most important people in your life.

	Name	Relationship
1.		
2.		
3.		
4.		
5.		
6.		
7.		

2. When you achieve the height of success who do you want to be by your side?
3. Do you have any personal relationships that are not currently in a healthy or good place?

Act NOW!

Time Limit: 10 Minutes

Mission:

- Do something nice or beneficial for one person on your list. Here are some ideas:

- Send a note, letter, email or text to say "You are awesome!"
- Buy them coffee or lunch.
- Invite them to an activity, outing, or date.
- Send flowers or candy.
- Make the call!
- Think of a way to make them laugh.

Homework:

1. Make a list of ways to strengthen the relationship between you and every person on your list.
    a. What do they need to hear you say about your relationship with them and the value of that relationship in your life?
    b. How can you show them that you care?

Get Connected:

- Be sure that you are Facebook Friends every person on your list.
- Invite at least three of your friends to join the H.E.R.O.I.C. movement!

DEFINING YOUR PURPOSE: IMPORTANT FACTORS

Several major factors must be considered when examining your purpose in life. The following is an examination of Time, Sacrifice, and The Three G's. Purpose provides a response to the greater of *why*. If you do not have that greater why then you are forced to endure the torture of punching a time clock in all activities: work, school, relationships, and in life.

TIME

Time is money.

Time is precious

Time marches on.

How do you spend your time? When you lay your head on the pillow at night, do you go to sleep with a full belly? Do you feel satisfied that you have wisely invested your time in yourself and others? Time is life's most valuable commodity. You can always get more money, property,

wealth and food. However, once the time is spent, it can never be recovered. In this sense, *time* has more value than money. We are only allotted a certain amount of time in our lives. Nothing can stop the flow of time. Once time is spent, it cannot be brought back by any means. Therefore the ultimate gift you can give is your time. Time is **SO** valuable, and we should ensure we use it wisely.

Unfortunately, most people do not realize the value of time and therefore squander it. Instead of focusing on important tasks at hand, they waste their time and mistakenly think they will make it up in the future.

> **You can always earn another dollar but once time is spent you will never get it back!**

Real heroes understand that many future troubles can be avoided by taking action in a prompt manner.

Cart Metaphor – One of my favorite illustrations for time is the Cart Metaphor. Imagine if all of your time and activities were represented by objects in a shopping cart. Many of us pack our

carts full with work, extracurricular activities, eating, sleeping, and family obligations. Before long there is no room for anything else (let alone time to catch your breath). What would happen if you unpacked your shopping cart and repacked it according to what matters in your life? What if you started by investing in yourself so that you had reserves and energy to then invest in other? What if you gave priority to establishing genuine Loving Profitable Relationships because you now have love, time and resources to share with others?

Heroes Use Time as a Key to Unlock Success

- **Time-management is a Matter of Priorities:** H.E.R.O.I.C. Time-management is a critical success factor. It is an important habit that lays the foundation for a fruitful future. For example, in the workplace, you should first do the hard things that make the most money or impact. Interestingly, studies have shown that the average employee only gives about 4-hours of solid work in the ordinary 8-hour day. What would it look like if you used the most brain power to work hard for 4-hours right when you arrived to work? In theory, if you make this a priority, you will accomplish the same amount of work in half the time. The same concept holds true in other areas of life as well. For instance, prioritizing *the important* in personal health. It has been scientifically proven that if you make time in the morning to work out, you will be more consistent and more efficient in your health regime. The point is to first carve out time for your priorities. Keep the main thing the main thing!

- **Punctuality:** Punctuality demonstrates a deep respect for both people and time. In a scheduled appointment, the late-comer usually gives an impression that they do not value the other person or their time. An H.E.R.O.I.C. person, who uses their time cautiously, becomes successful in life. It is easy to see that the successful people in all spheres of life make proper use of every moment. The most prosperous are those that do not waste a second. A person who is not punctual finds it difficult to finish their duties and ultimately sets themselves and coworkers up for failure. In the military field delay by a few minutes may change the destiny of a nation. Moment of Truth – I suck at this. The key is that I understand the value of this so much that I have hired someone to make sure that I am on time. They will text me 20 minutes before I need to be somewhere to ensure that I am not late. Someone with better discipline may be able to do this on their own. However, I know that this is an area of personal weakness so I delegate this responsibility to someone to ensure that I can meet my punctuality standards. If I am unable to follow-through I apply the Donut Moment Rule – if you are late, you better bring doughnuts. If you are not 15 minutes early, then you are late!

- **Value of Time:** Time has monetary value. Consider just a few of the following:
    1. We trade our time for money.
    2. In the military, you exchange your life for a set value.
    3. The more efficiently we work, the more money we can make.
    4. Interest on our savings will only accrue over time.
    5. If time is invested wisely today, the quality of tomorrow will be abundant.

People who understand the importance of time, work efficiently. In turn, this allows more time for additional tasks and goals. Throughout history, it is clear that successful people of history made the best use of time. Prosperous people are very conscious about the value of time. Hence, time should never waste, and everyone should try to make the best use of it.

Personal Reflection Questions:

1. What is currently in your shopping cart?

Item	Importance Scale: 1-10 (highest)
1.	
2.	
3.	
4.	
5.	
6.	
7.	
8.	
9.	
10.	

2. What do you need take out? Put back in?

   _____
   _____
   _____

3. What room are you leaving for yourself?

   _____
   _____
   _____

Act NOW!

Time Limit: 10 Minutes

Mission: What is something you know that you need to do, but you have been putting it off?

- Set the alarm for 10 minutes.
- Work on it until the alarm goes off. Even if you do not finish it, work on it!
- GO!!

Homework:

1. List three personal time-wasters.
    1. _____
    2. _____
    3. _____

2. What would you do if you had extra time in the day?
   _____

SACRIFICE

Every great storyline has universal themes. Some of the most important stories start with someone who is broken. Take for example *Braveheart*. He is a farmer. He is Drifting and does not know who he is. Then he has something taken from him, and he cannot get back. That unleashes a wildfire in him. He goes to prison and loses even more before it brings out his greater good. And only then can he ride fiercely into battle. But if you pay attention, he left a lot of things behind to get to that place. There was a sacrifice to live his H.E.R.O.I.C. life – there always is.

Sacrifice is to give something of value now to get something even more valuable in the future. The people in the world who achieve the most are often the ones who can sacrifice the most. Sacrifice is the beginning of the transition from Drifting to Driven. It is the thing that ultimately results in an achieving a Directed life.

Sacrifice is a natural part of life. This is especially true when trying to maintain a work-life balance. On the one hand, you need to provide the essentials (food and shelter) for you and your family. On the other hand, you need to invest time and attention into your family if you want to maintain familial ties. The key is to sacrifice enough so that you may provide for your family but not sacrifice too much that you lose them. Consider the following while processing life sacrifices.

- **If you do not stand for something, you will fall for anything.** To know how much you are willing to sacrifice, you must also have a clear understanding of lines that will never be crossed. Typically non-sacrificial items include:
    1. People or things that are too valuable to lose.
    2. Convictions regarding issues of integrity.

    For example, someone might sacrifice vast amounts of time and a personal life to get ahead in their workplace. However, they might draw the line at lying to the company or sleeping with their boss to get ahead. It is crucial that whatever is placed on the altar of success is something you are willing to lose forever.

- **Sacrifice always requires action with pure motives:** I could have anyone take a test about any aspect of the H.E.R.O.I.C. model, and they would say *"Absolutely, I need to have that area right in my life!"* The primary purpose is not to point out what you already know, but to ask what "you *doing* about it?" Even more importantly, it is to explain how your actions determine who you are. For example, you may say that you value your wife. But if you do not spend time with her or sacrifice for her, is that really true? Therefore, ultimately your actions reveal that you are not a good husband. But there is hope. There is a roadmap. One of the primary goals of the H.E.R.O.I.C. model is to bring actions and intentions into alignment. When accomplished, there is no limit to the success and fulfillment you can achieve!

- **Temporary Loss for Long-Term Reward:** Sacrifice always requires that you *lose something today* in exchange for *something better tomorrow*. The key is that the reward of tomorrow will be better than the temporary gain of today. For example, getting out of debt requires that you say no now for a greater yes later. Imagine, turning down little desires today will allow you to experience true freedom and greater pleasures tomorrow.

Personal Reflection Questions:

1. List 5 temporary enjoyments that you would be willing to sacrifice in order to reach your personal goals?

   1. _____
   2. _____
   3. _____
   4. _____
   5. _____

2. List 3 things that you are not willing to sacrifice in order to reach your goals.

   1. _____
   2. _____
   3. _____

Act NOW!

Time Limit: 10 Minutes

Mission: Give up something!

- Decide to give something up for 24 hours. Good for you. Bad for you. Big. Small. It can be anything!
- Find a friend, family member, co-worker or stranger and tell them what you selected.
- Start now and reassess in 24 hours.

Homework:

1. Reflect on what you decided to give up. Was it a positive item (something that added value to you or your life) or a negative item.

   _____
   _____
   _____
   _____
   _____

2. How did you feel after 24 hours?

   _____
   _____
   _____
   _____
   _____

Get Connected:

- Post a picture of the thing you gave up. #H.E.R.O.I.C.sacrifice

THE THREE G'S

Graciousness

Generosity

Gratitude

According to a phenomenal man, and my dear friend, Roy Mason, *The Three G's* are the best gift you can give to the world. The reason: it has to come from inside you. It is a decision that you make. *Graciousness, Generosity, and Gratitude* often come from a place of internal peace and personal contentment. For instance, if you are grateful internally you find ways to be grateful externally. If you are not, you will find reasons to be pessimistic. What if you made a conscious decision in life to show up with a thankful heart and a great attitude? What if you did not stop there? What if you were gracious because you have the opportunity, not the obligation, to serve those around you? How would life change for you and the people in your life?

I have such a newfound respect for *Graciousness, Generosity, and Gratitude*. In every situation, there is always some good and some bad. Imagine two people staring at the same valley. One can point out all of the shadows and obstacles. The other can see a great adventure and the light on the horizon. It is all about mindset. It is the filter through which you view the world and the people in it. Knowing that good exists in every situation, means that there is a significant choice to be made in the interplay of every circumstance. In every moment, there is something to be thankful for, an opportunity to be gracious and a chance to give.

For example, take something as mundane as going to eat at a restaurant. When you sit down at your table, and the server fills up your glass of water. Wow! I did not need to do anything, and a refreshment showed up. How cool is that! And when I finish and my cup is empty BAM new water magically shows up. I can choose to appreciate this water fairy and their efforts! I decide to have joy – even in a cup of water. Take a moment to let that sink in.

Imagine if you spent every week, day, hour, minute running your life through the filter of the *Three G's* – life would literally change.

1. **The Three G's come from a thankful heart.** Unfortunately, there is so much negativity and despair in the world today. These toxic thoughts and words are depressing, counterproductive and *not* H.E.R.O.I.C. The decision to be thankful changes negative inputs into productive and successful outputs. The processes of creating mantras and affirmations allow you to find ways to be grateful daily. You go from a life of complaining to a life of compassion and appreciation. Changing the narrative and tone of your personal story empowers you to create success in every area of your H.E.R.O.I.C. life.

2. **The Three G's strengthen relationships.** The moment I made gratitude, graciousness, and generosity a daily practice in my life, I noticed remarkable changes! My heart became more open towards others. I found myself being more compassionate. I was unshaken when things did not go according to plan. Most of all, I was able to process my experiences differently and find the good in a variety of people and relationships. Rather than focusing on the little things that bother

me about people, I made a conscious effort to look at their positive traits. I was gracious when others wronged me, and I searched for things to be thankful for. The Three G's filter strengthens bonds with others.

3. **The Three G's lead to a healthier life.** Research has shown that caring has tangible benefits for all involved. People who volunteer or care for others consistently tend to have better psychological well-being. This includes fewer depressive symptoms and higher life-satisfaction. Better relationships and a better outlook on life have proven to reduce blood pressure, decrease heart disease and even helps individuals meet their weight goals.

4. **The Three G's make you stand out.** If you want to be successful in the military, or in life, be the opposite of the status quo. The typical military profile is as follows: Go to work. Get drunk. Get girls. Repeat. Or if you are a family person: Go to work. Get home. Work more. Repeat. The problem is that a majority of people do this same routine over and over and their attitude adds to the

monotony and drudgery. People turn into sad robots. Choosing to be thankful allows an opportunity to look for new and exciting things to appreciate and enjoy. It is an attractive and rare quality! Others will notice. Therefore, if you want to get that date, earn that promotion, make that 50th anniversary or have more meaningful friendships put the Three G's into practice every day.

5. **The Three G's produce a more meaningful life.** When it comes to life meaning, nothing compares to living a life of gratitude, generosity, and graciousness. The Three G's filter provides purpose and passion. Being grateful will give you meaning because it allows you to capture the full essence of every moment. It takes the burden out of life while adding a dimension of beauty. It will enable you to find contentment even in moments of crisis. The Three G's will change you into a peaceful, conscious, and sacrificial person. You will be able to be present and live in the flow of life.

Personal Reflection Questions:

1. List 5 things that you are thankful for today.
   1. _____
   2. _____
   3. _____
   4. _____
   5. _____

2. When was the last time you gave something away?
3. Was it something of value or was it junk? How did it make you feel?

Act NOW!

Time Limit: 5 Minutes

Mission: Remind Yourself!

- Write a note to yourself that says "The Three G's: Graciousness, Gratitude, and Generosity."

- Put your reminder someplace that you will see it often (above bed, bathroom mirror, locker, etc.)
- Pick one of the G's and put it into action in the next 5 minutes.

Homework:

1. Think of the most positive person you know. How does being around that person make you feel? Practice being gracious and let them know what you think about them.

_____
_____
_____
_____
_____

2. What are some practical ways to show that you are thankful?

_____
_____
_____
_____
_____

Get Connected:

Post a picture or list of something you are thankful for # HEROICgratitude

IT IS NOT MONEY THAT MATTERS, IT IS HOW YOU USE IT THAT DETERMINES IT'S TRUE VALUE.

-UNKNOWN

Becoming H.E.R.O.I.C.

H.E.R.O.I.C.

CHAPTER TWO:

ENTREPRENEUR MINDSET

DRIFTING:
Unaware of personal finances and debt.

DRIVEN:
Desire to build financial wealth at any cost.

DIRECTED:
Strive to be financially responsible in order to share holistic wealth with others.

PRACTICAL STEPS TO BUILDING WEALTH

One primary element of an H.E.R.O.I.C. life is the ability to invest responsibly in your future. While there is a financial component to this methodology, having an entrepreneurial mindset has very little to do with money and everything to do with attitude and actions. A real hero is not hampered by financial ignorance or lack of assets because they made a series of daily choices that have built wealth over time and used their resources to invest in themselves and others.

Before my military experience, I had no training about money or the concept of building wealth. As a result, I squandered so much and lost everything! When I got out of the military and started making more of it, I knew I needed to consult experts. Amazing men intervened: Rick Ruby, Todd Scrima, Brian Kludt, Carson Vaughn, and Kevin Klieser. Below is a summary of the things I have gleaned over the years. If I had known about this system while I was in the military, I could have made SO much money with relatively no effort! Please take these lessons and apply them as soon as possible!

Also please note that the beautiful thing about this system is that it works. It does not matter if you are working your first job and making $30,000/year or if you are a multimillionaire.

> **THE SOONER YOU START, THE MORE MONEY YOU WILL MAKE!**

Many people make their financial system so complicated they never follow their plan! The purpose of this chapter is to lay out practical steps that work. Submit yourself to the following process, and I guarantee you will see results!

WEALTH-BUILDING STRATEGY

> **RULE #1 – KEEP IT SIMPLE!**

Step 1 – Track Everything

- **Three Main Accounts**
  1. Checking – Pay bills only
  2. Savings – Personal Allowance/ATM
  3. Money Market – (Survival Fund)

Step 2 – Be Consumer Debt Free

- Average credit card rate is 17%.
- Credit Card Company charges a usage fee.
- Maximum credit card interest: 27%.
- Invest in your consumer debt first!

Step 3 – Build a Survival Account

- Minimum payments needed to pay bills.
- Survival Account – This should be equal to three months' worth of minimum bills and expense.

Step 4 – Maximize your retirement savings

- Start with these ASAP to allow for the maximum benefits from compound interest.
- Roth IRA $5,500.00 maximum per year (additional $1,000/year if age = 50 years)
- 401k Company Match $18,000 maximum annual contributions
- If you are over 50 years of age, your maximum annual contribution is $24,000.
- SEP (Self Employed Pension Fund) maximum $53,000 per year.

Step 5 – Invest in the market

- This offers the most diversified strategies when investing in the stock market.
- Pick a diversified Mutual Fund
- Pick two different mutual Funds.
- Invest monthly (i.e., Dollar Cost Averaging)
- Create an account for your children or their education, like a 529 Plan

Step 6 – Pre-pay your mortgage

- When making a monthly mortgage payment, always round up to the nearest whole amount and pay extra.
- Last savings strategies employed
- Return on Investment = Interest Rate (5% Mortgage Interest Rate = 5% Return on Investment).
- Shorter term mortgages should be considered if you are not disciplined to prepay

Personal Reflection Questions:

1. Do you successfully do the following:

    - ☐ Track Everything
    - ☐ Consumer Debt Free
    - ☐ Built a Survival Account
    - ☐ Save for Retirement
    - ☐ Invest in the Market

Act NOW!

<u>Time Limit</u>: 10 Minutes

<u>Mission</u>: Personal Assessment!

- How much money do you currently have?

    - Checking = _____
    - Savings = _____
    - Money Market = _____
    - Survival Account = _____

Homework:

- If you were unable to accurately complete the "Act NOW!" schedule a meeting with a financial advisor or a true broker/planner – avoid the local banks and credit unions.

DANGER OF DEBT

Debt is a significant problem in the general population. On average, the typical American has $135,924 of debt. We typically owe $29,058 on our cars alone. The average family owes over $16,425 in credit card debt. As a culture, we are conditioned to excuse debt, or worse, expect it. This debt mindset is dangerous for anyone; however, this has severe repercussions for people in military service. There is NO reason that any person in the military should be in debt. You are heroes and not indentured servants! Avoiding foolish debt is H.E.R.O.I.C. and ensures personal and financial freedom.

	Total Owed by Average U.S. Household	Total Debt Owed by U.S. Consumers
Credit cards	$16,425	$764 billion
Mortgages	$180,018	$8.63 trillion
Auto loans	$29,058	$1.17 trillion
Student loans	$50,868	$1.34 trillion
Any type	$135,924	$12.73 trillion

Few people are aware that excessive debt also has the potential to impact your military career severely. The penalty for flagrant debt includes bad conduct discharge, forfeiture of all pay and allowances, and or 6-months of confinement. These charges apply if being in debt leads to acts of deceit or negligence.

> **DEBT → LOSS OF PRIVILEGES → ACTS OF DESPERATION → LOSS OF FREEDOMS**

Unfortunately, a majority of people *silently* carry the weight of debt. They only *feel* the pain of debt when they are directly and tangibly affected by the consequences. For example, if someone is cannot: purchase a home, get out of the military due to finances, buy an engagement ring or make a buy something because a credit card is declined.

I do many loans for the military, and almost every person that comes in has a considerable amount of debt. For example, a client has a car payment = $1,000. He makes $3,800/month. His car payment is over a third of his total income. That is not healthy. He is a debt prisoner!

Being in the military is a gift. As your term comes to an end (whether you signed up for four years, eight years, or 20 years) one of the most significant issues is *CAN I get out?* Many people in the military face questions regarding their uncertain future following their service. When they leave, they will no longer have a job and stable income. They typically need to reestablish themselves and their life. However, when they are looking down the barrel of a ton of debt, ultimately people end up staying in the military because they do not have the *choice.* That is the worst situation. Service to one's country should always be a choice.

Not *all* debt is bad! Some ventures require you go into debt. However, these are investments! Money that is spent and squandered is called debt. Money that is spent and yields something more significant is an investment. If there is a short-term loan or financial obligation that will yield a long-term gain (and it will prove more beneficial than savings), it should be considered. However, gambling money for the sake of quick returns will only lead to instability and long-term hardship.

Personal Reflection Questions:

- Do you have any of the following debts? If so how much?

  ☐ Y ☐ N Credit Cards _____

  ☐ Y ☐ N Auto Loans _____

  ☐ Y ☐ N Student Loans _____

  ☐ Y ☐ N Mortgages _____

  ☐ Y ☐ N Any Other Debt Type _____

Act NOW!

Time Limit: 10 Minutes

Mission: You have ten minutes to make some money! Find something to sell to a buddy, return a recently purchased item, ask a friend for a dollar or pick a penny off of the road.

- Now put that money (no matter how small) in a prominent place to serve as a reminder that a little effort yields positive results!

Homework:

- Have you made any financial investments? Will these investment yield more than simply saving the money with interest?

  _____
  _____
  _____
  _____
  _____
  _____

- Describe your plan to get out of debt?

  _____
  _____
  _____
  _____
  _____
  _____

Get Connected:

Post a picture or message sharing how much you were able to save or pay off in the last month #HEROICdeptdestroyer

PARTICULAR MONEY PIT FALLS IN THE MILITARY

I had a sailor in my office earlier today. He has three cars, two motorcycles, and three street bikes. He makes $3,200/month. Is that practical? I make a great deal more than he does every year and that is not practical for me! What on earth is this young man thinking?

Star Cards - The military comes with certain perks. One is the ability to obtain credit cards designed specifically for members of the Armed Forces. A majority of these credit cards do not require any qualification, merely an application. As a result, someone with poor credit or poor spending habits can easily outspend their next paycheck with an easy swipe. It is insane, I mean INSANE, how much people spend using these Star Cards. For the sake of your credit and your future, I would highly recommend avoiding the Star Card.

Cars – Cars are the single most significant money suck for military personnel! Not only do they lose value incredibly fast (see diagram below), but a majority of people in the service spend so much time away from their homes, they rarely get to enjoy their car. When I lived in a military dorm, all of the balconies faced a centralized parking lot. We would sit in our galleries and look at the cars parked below. These vehicles would be $50,000 trucks and "pimped out" cars with body kits! Guys, between ages 18 and 25, would be driving cars that their parents could not even afford after working and saving for thirty years.

Work the Lemon Lot – Buy USED! The standard car loses approximately 25% of the original value in the first year of ownership. That means when you go to a dealership and spend $33,560 (the average price of a new car). As soon as you drive off the lot, you have lost about $3,500! In five years, not including the cost of maintenance, you have now lost nearly 63% of the entire value of the car. That is $20,000 in the course of a typical term of service! Instead, buy used cars and pay cash. Let someone else absorb the depreciation and avoid a monthly payment.

Shane McGraw

HOW MUCH DO NEW CARS DEPRECIATE?

$33,560
The average cost of a new car in 2017.

$29,868
Just by driving off the lot, the car decreases in value by 11%.

$25,170
After one year, the car decreases in value by 25%.

$18,122
After three years, the car decreases in value by 46%.

$12,417
After five years, the car decreases in value by 63%.

Food – For many branches of the military a food allowance is either given or taken from your monthly paycheck. As a result, it makes the most sense to avoid eating outside of the places that provide food you are already purchasing. Another must-follow-money-saving-tip: buy groceries and prepare meals – cheaper, healthier, and leftovers!

FUTURE MILLIONAIRE: THE POWER OF SAVING

When I was in the military, DVDs were big. People would go to the BX and spend $400 on DVDs and movies. Why? We did not need those. We would watch them once or twice and never again. It was such a waste. I know because I collected them! Now fast-forward, if 20-year-old Shane had used his monthly DVD money and placed that in savings I could have turned $16,000 into almost $100,000! This is how $16,000 of shit cost me nearly $100,000 only ten years later!

All soldiers can become millionaires! If the average 20-year-old military person chooses to put away less than $200/month (less than $50/week!) during their time in the military – they can have a million dollars by the age of 50. By the age of 64 – over 2 million dollars! Here is how.

Age	Soldier A		Soldier B	
19	2,000	2,240	0	0
20	2,000	4,749	0	0
21	2,000	7,558	0	0
22	2,000	10,706	0	0
23	2,000	14,230	0	0
24	2,000	18,178	0	0
25	2,000	22,599	0	0
26	2,000	27,551	0	0
27	0	30,857	2,000	2,240
28	0	34,560	2,000	4,749
29	0	38,708	2,000	7,558
30	0	43,352	2,000	10,706
31	0	48,554	2,000	14,230
32	0	54,381	2,000	18,178
33	0	60,907	2,000	22,599
34	0	68,216	2,000	27,551
35	0	76,802	2,000	33,097
36	0	85,570	2,000	39,309
37	0	95,383	2,000	46,266
38	0	107,339	2,000	54,058
39	0	120,220	2,000	62,785
40	0	134,646	2,000	72,559
41	0	150,804	2,000	83,506
42	0	168,900	2,000	95,767
43	0	189,168	2,000	109,499
44	0	211,869	2,000	124,879
45	0	237,293	2,000	142,104
46	0	265,768	2,000	161,396
47	0	297,660	2,000	183,004
48	0	333,379	2,000	207,204
49	0	373,385	2,000	234,308
50	0	418,191	2,000	264,665
51	0	468,374	2,000	298,665
52	0	524,579	2,000	336,745
53	0	587,528	2,000	379,394
54	0	658,032	2,000	427,161
55	0	736,995	2,000	480,660
56	0	825,435	2,000	540,579
57	0	924,487	2,000	607,688
58	0	1,035,425	2,000	682,851
59	0	1,159,676	2,000	767,033
60	0	1,298,837	2,000	861,317
61	0	1,454,698	2,000	966,915
62	0	1,629,261	2,000	1,085,185
63	0	1,824,773	2,000	1,217,647
64	0	2,043,746	2,000	1,366,005
65	0	**2,288,996**	2,000	**1,532,166**

As you can see on this chart, Soldier A started saving $2,000 every year until he turned 26. At that time he stopped contributing money to this account! At that time Soldier B decided to start a savings investment. He added $2,000 every year until he turned 65 years old.

Soldier A turned almost $16,000 into nearly 2.3 million dollars. Soldier B had to put away $114,000, and he still came out behind!! By starting eight years earlier, Soldier A was able to let compound interest do the work and was ready to retire with almost twice as much as Soldier B.

THE EARLIER YOU START SAVING, THE MORE MONEY YOU MAKE!

The following two graphs demonstrate the power and importance of starting to save early. The first figure shows the total savings accrued by two individuals: Emily and Dave. Both individuals put the same amount of money into a savings account. The only difference is that Emily started saving ten years before Dave. The second graph displays the amount of money needed every month to have one million dollars at retirement. The amount varies depending on when saving starts.

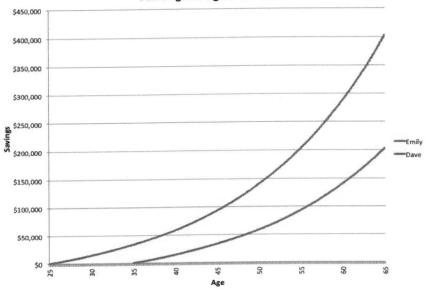

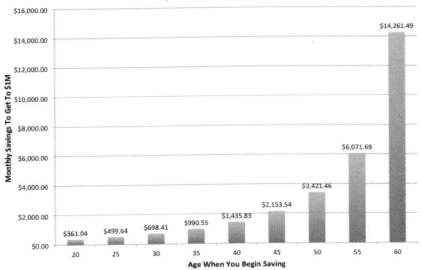

AUTOMATE THE IMPORTANT

Automating the important is an essential step in *all* areas of life. For instance, Date Night with your spouse. If you know that occurs every Wednesday at 7 o'clock in the evening; it has become automated. You have made an effort to ensure that investing in your relationship is a priority. This concept is particularly real for managing personal finances. The military has a process called *allotments*. It is a way to tell Uncle Sam where to send your money before you ever see your paycheck. Using this system allows you to send money to specific accounts of your choosing. Smart people take time to ensure priorities are automated. Please consider making contributions to the following before you ever see your paycheck:

1. An "out of sight, out of mind" savings account. (Money Market)

2. A Thrift Savings Plan (TSP) account for retirement savings – not because it is necessarily the best but because of the match.

3. An Individual Retirement Account (IRA) in order to maximize returns.

Personal Reflection Questions:

1. List 5 financial goals.

    1. _____

    2. _____

    3. _____

    4. _____

    5. _____

2. Consider the Five Financial Commandments for Military Personnel. How are you doing?

    1. Spend Basic Housing Allowance (BHA) Wisely.

    2. Never be in debt (more than 40% of "bring home" pay).

    3. Save all signing bonuses and special pay (for your entire military career).

    4. Work the Lemon Lot until you have been in the military for at least ten years.

    5. Automate Every paycheck – 10% to savings and 10% to giving.

Act NOW!

<u>Time Limit</u>: 10 Minutes

<u>Mission</u>: Check Yourself!

- Look at the charts above. Based on your age and income, how much do you need to put aside to have a million dollars before retirement? _____
- Log into your bank account and see how much liquid cash you have available.
- Log into your accounts and see how much money you have in your retirement.
- What should you keep the same?
- What should you automate?

Homework:

1. Set up your automated system. If you already have one, check to ensure everything is constant with your financial goals.

Get Connected:

- Post a picture or message stating one financial goal and what you will do to celebrate reaching that goal! #IgotsomeHEROICdreams

GOD GAVE YOU *TWO* EARS AND *ONE* MOUTH SO YOU SHOULD PROBABLY LISTEN TWICE AS MUCH AS YOU TALK

AN OLD IRISH PROVERB

H.E.R.O.I.C.

CHAPTER THREE:

RELATIONSHIPS

DRIFTING:
My relationships are about "?".

DRIVEN:
My relationships are about "Me".

DIRECTED:
My relationships are about "We".

UNIVERSAL TRUTHS

Relationships are hard. Even when they are right and healthy, they are hard. And when relationships are excellent they are even harder. Good! You are a hero. You thrive on hard things! While I was reflecting on this section, my wife and I happened to get into an argument. I knew that I was right and I did not understand *why* she was responding to me in that way. I turned to walk away. I was thinking, "when you are ready to stop treating me this way, and after you admit that you are wrong, I will talk with you." As I was leaving the room, I had the thought "Be H.E.R.O.I.C." I turned around, with a gritty act of my will I proclaimed, "Dang it! I am going to be the hero of my story". I turned around and calmly approached my wife. I told her that I did not understand her responses, but I love her, so I want to know her. I asked if she could help me understand. It turned out that she was upset about something else entirely. It had nothing to do with me. If I had just walked out of the door, I would have missed out on the opportunity to learn about my wife and her pain. By giving up my right to be right, I loved my wife and grew a little closer to her. Yes, it cost me something. I had to die to my selfishness and the fact that I had not done anything! I had to choose to see past my desire to be right, and I had to look to her needs. However, the payout from that momentary investment yielded tremendous rewards to us both. *I* was H.E.R.O.I.C., and *we* both won!

BE INDEPENDENTLY HEALTHY: THE "H STORY"

I attended pre-marriage counseling with my wife before our wedding. In one of our sessions, our counselor told us to view marriage a Capitol A. Many describe their relationship as leaning on one another and sharing mutual life goals and interests. However, this is an unhealthy and incorrect view of relationships. Rather an H.E.R.O.I.C. relationship should look like this:

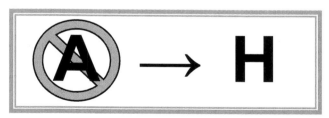

A= Co-dependency H = Healthy and Independent

The image depicts two healthy individuals that stand independently. Only then may their shared passions be mutually uplifting. When individuals are capable of standing on their own, then they are free to be connected and supportive of one another. Unfortunately, too many of my friends try to keep their wives "dumb and in the kitchen." They try to force their partner into total reliance. Consequently, they typically default to enforcing "traditional roles" which may not be in their partner's wheelhouse.

I want my wife to be able to pick up the ball and run if I fall – and vice versa. I push her to do hard things, and she drives me. We strive to be the best versions of ourselves independently, and then we urge one another to move out of our respective comfort zones. We are best friends in that regard. We push each other, and then we celebrate the victories of our partnership. Often our society encourages us to force the other person to be dependent on us. But if we do this, we are both shaky, unstable, and incomplete versions of ourselves. Ultimately we both lose.

There are no clear lines in relationships. However, there are some self-evident truths. To be in a healthy relationship, we must first unpack what is necessary to be a healthy individual.

VULNERABILITY

To be in any lasting relationship, it requires one to put themselves in a position of vulnerability. It mandates that a person opens up and lets someone into their inner world. It is a sacred trust. Often if someone has been hurt in life, they can never move beyond this first step. As a result, this person will be stuck with negative emotions and a series of self-indulging, short, broken relationships. When the relationship requires any sacrifice that is "not worth it" the relationship ends. The figures below compare two different ways of relating, whether it be a spouse, friend or co-worker. The first image results in a cycle of unhealthy relating. The second figure shows an efficient way to break the dysfunctional cycle and more toward H.E.R.O.I.C. relationships.

Vicious Cycle

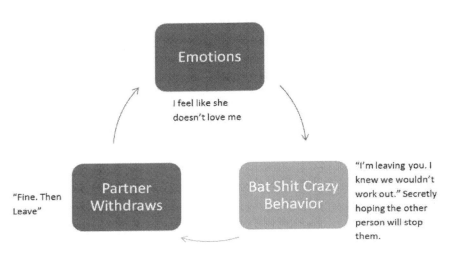

Healthy Cycle

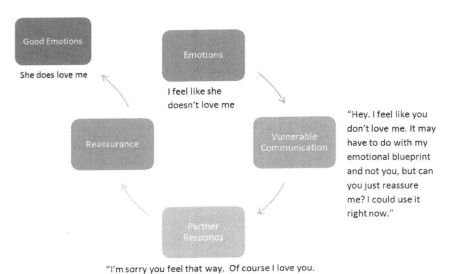

EXPECT NOTHING – BE GRATEFUL FOR EVERYTHING

The fastest way to kill any relationship and leave you broken-hearted: misplaced expectations. The belief that something will happen or should happen. The number one piece of advice I give people, if you have expectations of anyone or anything, you are setting yourself up for resentment. As soon as you have enforced aspirations of someone else you are giving them an opportunity to fail. No one person or situation can be everything you want, desire or need. The best gift you can give your friends or family is not to have any expectations of them, just love them. For example, I saw my father three years ago, and he kept trying to call me *son* and play like a father. I eventually told him *we could be buddies but not father and son. That shit passed a long time ago.* After all the pain and hurt that man caused me, it would be so easy to carry anger and bitterness around. However, although he did not fulfill the expectations of a good father does not mean that I can use those unrealized expectations to be a horrible person myself. Ultimately, I need to adjust my expectations, make a choice to let go, and make the H.E.R.O.I.C. effort to move on.

If you are going to have expectations in life, have them of yourself. Set your sights high but practice being gracious with yourself. There will always be someone better. But if you give your best, in all things, it is hard to leave disappointed.

Guidelines for Developing Personal Expectations:

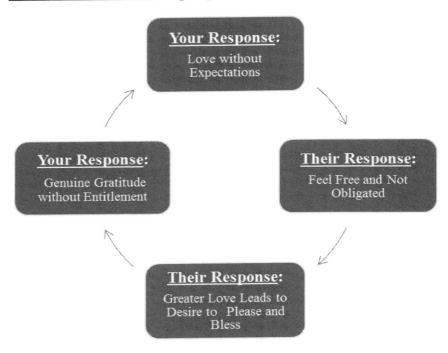

1. **With Others:** Expect Nothing, Be Grateful for Everything – While not an absolute rule, if you adopt this mindset every day, it will change your life. It will allow you an opportunity just to love and appreciate those around you. As a result, they will be free to love you in return.

When they do something that blesses or benefits you get to respond with genuine gratitude and love.

2. **With Yourself:** Aim high, Attack Fiercely, Respond Graciously!
   - <u>Aim high</u> – Do not just settle for the bare minimum. Push yourself towards greatness.
   - <u>Attack Fiercely</u> – Once you have your goals set, pursue them with all the vigor of tenacity of a lion stalking their prey
   - <u>Respond Graciously</u> – Win or lose!
     - *During Successful* – Celebrate! Positive affirmations (especially self-affirmations) trigger a chain reaction in the brain that releases hormones that improve mood and memory. When you give yourself credit, your mind wants to do it again. Give yourself credit for being successful, and you are more apt to repeat success.
     - *During Failure* – Failure = opportunity. Do not fall into the trap of self-pity or loathing. Acknowledge disappointment and give yourself space to process those feelings. Do not linger! Use that time to learn and deepen your resolve!

Personal Reflection Questions:

1. List five expectations you have.
2. Are these expectations of other people or of yourself. How can you turn your expectations of others into higher expectations of yourself?

Expectations	Circle One
1.	You or Others
2.	You or Others
3.	You or Others
4.	You or Others
5.	You or Others

Turn It On Yourself
1.
2.
3.
4.
5.

Act NOW!

Time Limit: 10 Minutes

Mission: Turn expectations into love!

- Think about the person (other than yourself) that you expect the most from – a friend, spouse, child, employee, co-worker. Who have you imposed expectations on?
- Think about how you are going to reclaim those expectations. Say out loud "From now on, I am going to own that."
- Show your love – Think of a way to show that person that you love and care about them. Do It – with no expectations of anything in return!

Get Connected:

- Post a picture or message stating your commitment to no more expectations! Post a picture that includes the words "No more expectations!"

TYPES OF RELATIONSHIPS

BROTHERHOOD

One of the most significant gifts in the military is the comradery. Everything the military is centered around covering your buddy's six, "never leave a man behind" and "I did it for my brothers." There are so many incredible stories and storylines that feature someone doing something extraordinary for their fellow man. We are trained to be that way in a time of war. However, when things are peaceful, we are awful to one another. I mean you think that bullying in high school is terrible! It is nuts! I am talking about: pissing on each other in the shower, whipping each other with towels, and playing massive pranks. It gets to the point where people need psychological counseling to cope with some of the stuff that happens. To complicate matters, in many instances hierarchy comes into play. There is a mindset that *I have a higher rank, so I can treat you how the Hell I want*. Unfortunately, most people are missing out on an incredible opportunity to develop life-long friendships and relationships.

Something happens when you eat, sleep, work, play, develop, watch sports and live together. You are never going to be that close with someone again. Now if you get married or have a long-term relationship with someone, it might come close. However, these dynamics are different because that is a romantic relationship. It would be incredibly rare to have a situation where you get the opportunity to live in such proximity with friends. Relationships built during this season are gold. To this day I am still friends with a handful of my military buddies. However, had I known the incredible potential of these relationships for future networking and lifelong relationship, I would have invested way more into these individuals. Without a doubt, it is the secret sauce of your time during the military – the people.

Personal Reflection Questions:

1. Think about the buddies in your circle of friends. List the following three things about each of them (hometown, career aspirations following the military, and personal interests). Now consider the networking possibilities!

    1. _____
    2. _____
    3. _____
    4. _____
    5. _____

Act NOW!

Time Limit: 10 Minutes

Mission: Bro Date!

- Organize a get together for you and your friends. Something that is positive, out of the box, adventurous and will lead to a year's worth of stories! Go make a remarkable memory with your buds!

SEX AND WOMEN

My time in service was about working, drinking beer and women. Women. And more Women. The focus of our world was on who could drink the most beer and have sex with the most women. Furthermore, Uncle Sam ships you to foreign countries where women are not held in high regard. As a result, outside of almost every international base, there is a whorehouse. Interactions with the opposite gender are inevitable. *How* these transpire will make all the difference for both individuals. The H.E.R.O.I.C. approach results in mutual benefit rather than exploitation. This shift turns the focus from casual consumption into intentional investment.

The best advice I can give on this topic is to present an honest reflection about how I sucked at all of this and what I learned as a result. While in the military, there is an opportunity to meet people from all over the world. Every single race, ethnicity,

> **THE H.E.R.O.I.C. APPROACH FOCUSES ON MUTUAL BENEFIT RATHER THAN EXPLOITATION.**

size, shape, and personality. Rather than consume them – enjoy them. There is a difference. I am not suggesting that you enter a long-term commitment with every person. Instead, I am proposing a shift in thinking. Enjoy the company and fellowship of others rather than just looking for a notch on a bedpost.

I was in Vegas before I was deployed to the Middle East. It was a lonely time of drinking, smoking and lots of women. My buddies and I would get gussied up and hit the strip looking for as many women to consume as possible. Whether we were lucky on our quest or not, we would always come back lonely. We never learned how to enjoy and not just consume. These are people. How will the interaction they have with you affect their life? Will it be life-giving for them or life-sucking? These were never considerations for me. As a result, I was never satisfied.

A buddy of mine could tell that was in a cycle that was leading nowhere. With this pending deployment, he suggested that I take a season to focus on myself. I agreed. Little did I know that my three-month stint would turn into nine months! It was a hard, and much needed, time of no drinking, smoking or women. Instead, I focused on getting to know me. I read, learned, and spent time getting to *know* other people. As I learned about myself, I came to see that had been trying to fill a hole that could never be filled by another person. The result was a lot of wasted energy and useless heartache. Only after I returned from that time, did I understand how to be a man worthy of a woman.

This will sound crazy, but if I could do it again, I would suggest not dating for the first five years in the military. Instead use that time to invest in yourself – save your money, get your body and mind right, learn your craft. Only then will you be in a position where you can present yourself to another person who is worthwhile.

Personal Reflection question:

1. How would your relationship with the opposite gender change if you looked for ways to enjoy them rather than use them for personal fulfillment?

THE THIRTY YEAR FRIEND

Friendship is a word that we use freely and apply loosely within our culture. They say that the average adult has no more than two or three best friends. Remember the adage, "if you go into the word looking for friends you will find few if you set out to be a friend you will have an abundance." Therefore you should focus your time doing right by others. Do not have any expectations in return and then gratefully enjoy the return on your investment.

Love requires actions. Friendship requires actions. There is a level of selflessness and sacrifice that comes from doing life with someone. One of the best things I have heard regarding friendship was a talk entitled, "The Thirty Year Friend." It changed the way that I selected friends and invested in those bonds.

> **IS THIS FRIENDSHIP WORTH THE 30-YEAR INVESTMENT THAT I WILL NEED TO MAKE? IF YES, PURSUE IT WITH EVERYTHING YOU HAVE!**

First, I took an inventory of the people in my life and asked the following questions:

1. Is this person someone that will be a benefit to my life for the long haul?

2. Is that friendship worth the investment that I will need to make?

If the answer is yes to both these questions, then it is necessary to ensure the building blocks are in place so that relationship grows and that it is *mutually* profitable. Below are some H.E.R.O.I.C. guidelines for developing and sustaining lasting friendships that will thrive through the various phases and pressures of life.

- **Permit yourself to be vulnerable.** Give trusted friends the opportunity and permission to speak both positively and negatively in your life. Understanding that they know things about you that you may not even know about yourself. Being open and vulnerable to trusted critique benefits you and your friendship in the long run.

- **It is okay not to be friends with everybody.** You cannot let the praises or criticisms of another define you as a person.

Yes, compliments and words of encouragement are excellent and make you feel good. But if who you are as a person is dependent on the praises of another you will change yourself to accommodate and impress others. That is not healthy. In the same way, if someone criticizes you it is essential to learn from feedback but not devalue yourself.

- **Allow for the seasons of life.** Each season of life comes with benefits and challenges. These are a natural and healthy reality. For instance, career pursuits, child-rearing, empty-nesters, and care of elderly family members. Individuals respond differently to these seasons: some thrive, and others struggle. Be patient and supportive during the periods that are hard for your friends and learn from them when they are succeeding.

- **Speak the truth in love.** A true friend will tell you what you *need* to hear not what you *want* to hear. They are the ones to say *"Dude you suck with money, let me help you."* Or *"Hey you are an ass today is everything okay?"* Be able to tell your friends the truth and be able to receive it like a hero!

Personal Reflection Questions:

1. How would your relationships look differently if you selected your friends based on a life-long friendship?

   _____
   _____
   _____
   _____
   _____
   _____
   _____
   _____
   _____

2. Who are your closet friends?

   1. _____

   2. _____

   3. _____

   4. _____

   5. _____

Act NOW!

Time Limit: 10 Minutes

Mission: Call or text one of your friends just to say "Hey, I am thinking about you."

Homework:

1. Reflect on your "Five Closest Friends" list. What season of life are they in? Think of two things you can do to meet them where they are at, lend a helping hand, or encourage them.

Get Connected:

- Post a picture of something you did to encourage a friend. #myHEROICfriendships

MARRIAGE

Marriage is one of the most important relationships. It has the potential to serve as a lifeline and support for any storm in life. Unfortunately very few would describe their current marriage as good, let alone great. As a result, these unions can become a massive anchor that weakens morale, hinders progress and ultimate sinks the ship! To become an H.E.R.O.I.C. spouse, the following section will examine the following:

1. Overall Approach
2. Special Consideration for Service Members
3. Strengthening Marital Connections
4. Maintaining your Relationship
5. Fighting Fair
6. Resolving Conflict

Overall Approach

A couple of days before my first deployment, I made a deal with God. If I "got right," he would give me a wife. (Now, I realize I had no idea what it looked like to "get right"!) I expected God to give me a hot wife that met all my specifications. I started to see that it had nothing to do with that other person could bring to the table. It had everything to do with me. What type of person was I? I began to realize that I needed to be the person that was worthy of being married.

I have now been married for almost fourteen years and often think about that deal I made with God. Years of marriage reveal the faulty thinking I had when I made that deal. It is not about whether I can get the perfect women to be my wife. How can *I* be a better man for *her*! When you are given the gift of a spouse, you have the opportunity to spend the rest of your life being thankful.

> **WHEN YOU ARE GIVEN THE GIFT OF A SPOUSE, YOU HAVE THE OPPORTUNITY TO SPEND THE REST OF YOUR LIFE BEING THANKFUL.**

Selflessness is at the core of any H.E.R.O.I.C. relationship. Typically people enter a romantic relationship because of what they get out of it. It feels good. It boosts self-esteem. It provides satisfaction and fulfillment. That is infatuation, lust, or "love at first sight." It is incredible, but it fades. That type of relationship provides a temporary boost of love that is intense, but it disappears if there is nothing else to sustain it. Self-sacrifice and commitment provide the sustaining nourishment for lasting relationships.

For example, I enjoy having a good time and unwinding with my friends. However, I gave up drinking altogether about 11 months ago. It was a decision that I had to make for myself, but I knew that my wife did not deserve to have a drinker for a husband. I was not always a jerk but occasionally when I would wake up the next morning and need to apologize for something I said or did it is because alcohol was involved. Ultimately, the need for me to enjoy myself should not outweigh the hassle for my wife.

What are little things that you can stop doing or give up to make your spouse's life easier and more enjoyable?

SPECIAL CONSIDERATION FOR SERVICE MEMBERS

For H.E.R.O.I.C. service members, a loving, resilient marriage is both a matter of personal happiness and family readiness. When family relationships are strong and healthy, service members are free to focus on their mission and daily duty requirements. Marital problems related to deployment and military service can include, but are not limited to:

- Struggles related to service-caused PTSD, depression or anxiety.
- Caregiving challenges and adjustments if a service member is injured.
- Feelings of isolation or resentment on the part of a spouse at home.
- Infidelity related to long separations.
- The "rollercoaster effect" of the ups and downs related to deployment.

The following resources are intended explicitly for H.E.R.O.I.C. military couples to reduce the strain on their partnerships.

- The armed forces offer many helpful support programs for couples and families, including classes and retreats. Take advantage, even if you think you do not need them.
- Consciously work on ways to maintain your connection when apart, using tools like care packages, journal exchanges (my personal favorite), and sharing memories and goals.
- Reach out for assistance from friends (others going through the same thing may be helpful), family, and military programs.
- Educate yourself on the stages of deployment and typical reactions to these stages, so that you understand what is going on. It can be very comforting to realize that you are normal.

Being part of a military couple has its challenges. However, these marriages and spouses unquestionably also have their strengths. Together, you and your spouse can unite to face the challenges of remaining close while continuing to serve your country.

STRENGTHENING MARITAL CONNECTIONS

Good, rocky or somewhere in the middle, every H.E.R.O.I.C. relationship can benefit from tips, techniques, and resources to help you keep your bonds active and healthy. Strengthen your connection with these strategies:

- **Adjust your expectations** – Accept yourself, your spouse and your relationship as they exist today. It is natural to want the honeymoon to last forever. But people and relationships change over time. Each milestone brings new dynamics and routines. Use these unique seasons as an opportunity to learn, discover and grow. You, your spouse, and your marriage are continually evolving. Adopting a mindset of flexibility and positivity will make life easier.

- **Date Night** – How do two people that like one another get to know one another? They go on a date. Time together without distractions can remind you of what brought you together and rekindle the feelings when your relationship was just starting. The date also creates the necessary space to continue to learn about your spouse. Lastly, it provides an opportunity to make your time, attention, attitude and actions all about serving your spouse! The demands of life will ensure that "couple time" gets pushed to the back burner. Do not let this happen! Heroically fight for your time together – s*chedule* time. Your marriage is important enough to be a priority.

- **Take turns planning your activities** – Romance should be an ongoing part of your relationship, not just reserved for special occasions. Be thoughtful in your plans and consider what your spouse enjoys. Make your date about *them*!

- **Create rituals.** Routine and rituals can help hold a relationship together. A goodbye kiss before work, breakfast in bed with the crossword puzzle on weekends, weekly date nights, or a walk after dinner are the little things that count. This also includes helping your spouse with their tasks or chores.

MAINTAIN YOUR RELATIONSHIP

Just like our cars need maintenance, marriages need care to run smoothly and last a long time, too. Here are a few practical tips for a happy, high-mileage and H.E.R.O.I.C. marriage:

- **Take the pulse of your relationship.** Look carefully at your relationship. What is and is not working? Decide together on the compromises you are willing to make.

- **Discuss how much time you spend together.** Do you wish spending time together was a higher priority? Are you talking honestly and frequently about things that bother you? Discuss changes that will bring more harmony.

- **Make a habit of talking frequently.** Being in contact can keep you both connected. Some people use a phone call during the day to settle the family business, so they are free to enjoy time together when they get home.

- **Plan for roadblocks.** You will not always agree on everything. Think about and discuss situations you know cause friction, and plan to treat one another with respect before a disagreement happens.

- **Share household work.** Running the household together takes work by both partners. Be willing to work out who does what so you are both satisfied.

- **Give each other space.** Your relationship will be stronger and more interesting if you give your spouse time and space without you. Remember, one person cannot possibly meet all your needs. Both spouses must keep and nurture outside friendships and interests.

- **Do not talk badly about your spouse.** I had a buddy in the military who was married. His favorite pastime was to complain about his wife. He would say, "She puts the toilet paper on wrong…she never cleans out the car…she does not do dishes…" I used to think "Man your wife is both pleasing to the eye and she has a great heart. You cannot think of any way to be thankful for how awesome she is?" Fast forward almost fifteen years. Honestly, I wonder how many times I have been frustrated with my wife, and people have wondered the same thing about me! One of the greatest mistakes you can make in marriage is to speak poorly about your spouse. It makes you both look bad!

BE H.E.R.O.I.C: FIGHT FAIRLY

Conflicts and disagreements are a regular part of a healthy and H.E.R.O.I.C. marriage. The topic of dispute is less important than both of you being willing to fight fairly. Remember you are often fighting for the same things, just from different vantage points.

- **Do not say hurtful things when you fight.** It is hard to show restraint during an argument, but your discussion will be more productive if you express yourself without being mean-spirited.

- **Avoid Universal Statements.** You *always*... I *never*...*every* time...*All* such statement are counterproductive! These lead to hurt and defensive postures. When walls go up, there is more effort and less communication.

- **Debrief after a disagreement.** Talk about what happened when both of you have cooled off. Choose a time and place that is convenient for both spouses. Concentrate on hearing the other. This is important even after the conflict is resolved and the relationship is restored!

- **Be respectful.** LISTEN while your spouse expresses feelings and needs, and acknowledge them. Even if you disagree with everything that is coming out of their mouth.

- **Use "I" statements to express your feelings.** For example, try "I feel hurt when you leave the table without thanking me for cooking," instead of "you" statements, such as "You are selfish because you leave the table without saying thanks." "I" statements tend to open conversation. Whereas "you" statements tend to feel like an attack.

- **Focus on the issue at hand.** Avoid the temptation to resurrect events and evidence from your history as a couple. This is a *tough* thing to do (especially if this is not the first time that an offense has occurred). However, staying in the present will help resolution happen more efficiently.

HOW TO SOLVE CONFLICT

Learning to fight fairly is an imperative H.E.R.O.I.C. attribute. Learning to resolve conflict is another. Here are some ideas to help:

- **Trade off bad habits.** Small annoyances can cause big problems. Strike a deal: both drop a bad habit that bothers the other.

- **Remember your spouse's good qualities.** For every dirty dish left in the sink, your spouse likely has done a dozen wonderful things you could not live without. Get into the habit of looking for your spouse's positive traits – you will see less of the bad.

- **Notice and acknowledge what your spouse is doing for you and your family.** Daily saying "thanks" will remind you of your spouse's efforts; hearing it will make them feel valued.

Like any good relationship, marriages take work and attention. From rediscovering dating to intentional communication and navigating conflict, with a little effort, you can have an amazing and H.E.R.O.I.C. marriage.

Personal Reflection Questions:

1. Do you feel connected to your spouse? What could strengthen your bond?
2. How do you and your partner fight? Is it fair?
3. How do you and your partner resolve conflict?

Act NOW!

Time Limit: 10 Minutes

Mission: List 5 things that you love or appreciate about your spouse. Go tell them!

1. _____
2. _____
3. _____
4. _____
5. _____

Homework:

Congratulations! If you are reading this, you are the official Date Night Planner for this week! Have fun! Here are some rules:

- It does not need to be expensive! A hike, walk or picnic will do the trick!
- You must plan. Organize childcare, make reservations, or buy tickets. Remember the 5 Ps: Prior planning prevents piss-poor performance!
- Think about what *they* would like. What are their interests?

Get Connected:

- Post a picture of your Date Night to the H.E.R.O.I.C. page! #myhotHEROICdate!

PARENTING

Do Not Let Bad History Repeat Itself

Behind the house that I grew up in, there was an old Miniature Golf course, an abandoned warehouse, and a fish hatchery. During the day I got to play with these old things, shoot Beebe guns, play hide-and-seek. It was a surreal setting! This was a dramatic juxtaposition to how things were when I went home. My dad was very into drugs at that point. People were overdosing. We had head lice. There was a lot of bullying. He rejected me, and I desperately wanted his approval. My father's way of "approving of me" was beating me up. *You are not good enough. You should have done better.* It was his way of making me tougher, stronger, and manly. At ten years old you do not make your son manly. You teach them how to open doors for their mother, how to carry out the garbage or how to unload the groceries from the car. You do not yell at them and call them a pussy. That does not get them anywhere.

My kids are now older than I was when my father left. While I will never forget how my father treated me, I am now to a place where it does not define me. Now that I am older, I can see that he had a lot of expectations of the world and only saw life through his own eyes. Everything was about what he deserved, what he did not get, ways that the world had failed him. And I, I, I…. if I do not want to be that same parent to my children, I must choose to put their needs and wellness above my desires, wants, selfishness, pains, hurts, and past. Parenting is intended to be H.E.R.O.I.C., not selfish. It cannot be about using children to fill some hole from your childhood. That only perpetuates a cycle of pain and hurt.

What is Your Example?

With my kids, I know that one of my most significant roles is to be their mentor. That means sometimes I need to look my wife in the eye and say I got this. My job is to raise a child that has the building blocks to take into this world. There are moments that, as a parent, you have the opportunity, and it is your job, to build those blocks. To have the courage to parent your children that way, you need to do the work yourself. <u>Remember</u>: more is caught than taught! It all starts with your emotional intelligence, your daily discipline, all of the little things that make up the big things.

Why Don't you Just Smile?

The other day I was walking into the store, and I heard a mother berating her son. She said *when we get into the store you need to smile. You need to look happier.* I was wondering how she would respond if I said the same thing to her. As I was circling the store (I cannot navigate a store to save my life!), I kept running into these two. She continued to let him have it. *Are you finally going to smile? Are you smiling now?* I was thinking; you are asking your son to externally display emotions that oppose his inward feelings. What kind of parenting is that? Why not discover what is bothering him. Listen. Build trust. Nurture. Maybe then he will have a reason to smile.

A Special Note for H.E.R.O.I.C. Families

Bringing a child into this world during a time of service should not be taken lightly. Inherently, your service is going to pull you away. The number one requirement for effective parenting is time invested. However, the military will always win the battle for your time. Yes, the military tries to be good about giving your time, when the situation allows. But the government did not issue you a wife or a child. In the military, the mission comes first, always. So, if you want to have a family, you need to be prepared for the natural tensions and pending challenges that will occur. You are committing that child to a life of service as well. They are on the mission too. They will spend their time traveling from place to place. New schools. New sports. New friends. Therefore if you are going to do it, you need to make the "sense of home" about the people, not the places.

The amount of time military individuals spend away from their families is unreal. Unless you have experienced that, very few people have an appreciation of the sacrifice required. Children going from birth to their first birthday, kids going through puberty, children leaving to go to college. The truth is that time marches on and vast periods of life are lost forever.

The H.E.R.O.I.C. Family Protection Plan

The H.E.R.O.I.C. Family Protection Plan is a group of house guidelines that increase the health and wellness of the entire family structure and all individual members of the family. From infants to teens, the H.E.R.O.I.C. Family Protection Plan is suitable for every child and family. These factors build on your family's strengths and can easily be incorporated into your daily routine:

- **Nurture and attachment** – Research shows that simple acts of affection, such as hugs or loving words (useful for younger children) and listening to worries and being involved in activities (more effective for older children), have a significant impact on growth and development.

- **Knowledge of parenting and child development** – Take some of the stress out of parenting. Stay current on parenting and child development information to help you recognize your child's abilities and set realistic expectations for their behavior. Every child is unique, but a basic understanding of child development will ensure your life is easier.

- **Parental resilience** – The ability to recognize stress and deal with it healthily increases your well-being and shows your kids positive ways to cope. Recognize the signs of stress and distracted parenting.

- **Social connections** – Having a solid group of friends and family to help and give you advice can take the edge off a rough day and allow you to enjoy your family.

- **Social and emotional competence of *your* children** – The ability of your child to interact with the world makes a big difference in how they form relationships.

- **Concrete supports for parents** – Every family needs a support network in the community and at home to help overcome challenges. To do this, you need to KNOW your children. When was the last time you spent more time listening and asking questions?

The H.E.R.O.I.C. Family Protection Plan can be part of your every day, hectic family life, and they can have positive, lifelong effects on your family's happiness and well-being.

Personal Reflection Questions:

1. Do you feel connected to your children? What could strengthen your bond?
2. Do you know your individual children's current strengths, struggles, hopes and fears?

Act NOW!

Time Limit: 10 Minutes

Mission: Ask your children how you are doing as a parent. Provide a safe space for them to respond honestly.

Homework:

Organize a Family Date for some time this week! Have fun! Here are some rules:

- It does not need to be expensive!
- Leave technology at home – yes *everyone!*
- Think about what *they* would like. What are their interests?

Get Connected:

- Post one or two guidelines you have to keep your family happy, healthy, and wise! #myHEROICfamily

"WHAT IS THE MOST EXPENSIVE BED IN THE WORLD? A SICKBED. YOU CAN EMPLOY SOMEONE TO DRIVE THE CAR FOR YOU, MAKE MONEY FOR YOU BUT YOU CANNOT HAVE SOMEONE BEAR THE SICKNESS FOR YOU."

– STEVE JOBS

H.E.R.O.I.C.

CHAPTER FOUR:

OVERALL HEALTH

DRIFTING:
No Ownership of Health or Fitness

DRIVEN:
Health and Fitness Used for Selfish Gain

DIRECTED:
Health and Fitness Used to Benefit Others

OVERALL HEALTH

H.E.R.O.I.C. health has very little to do with actual physical health and more with how you feel about yourself. There are a lot of different body structures. Within those structures, there are various shapes, diverse fat content percentages, dissimilar metabolisms, and countless ways of gaining weight or losing weight. There are numerous studies about blood types and examining the how our outward appearance is determined. But, in truth, the primary factor determining health is food. What fuels your engine? What do you put in your body, how much, and when? Admittedly, I am not very good at healthy eating myself. Every six months, I revert to my chubby kid eating habits. What I have learned in the struggle of going from fat to thin and back again is that I feel much better when I am healthy. If you are not healthy, the rest of your life does not work right. Think about it:

- Your mind
- Your self-esteem
- Your home life
- Your energy level
- Your work day

They are all directly impacted by the choice to be healthy. It is impossible to be H.E.R.O.I.C. if these areas are not working the way they should. When I was younger, I did not realize the impact that health has on the overall quality of life. (Few young people understand this correlation because they are typically healthy and in the prime of their lives.) If you ask an elderly couple what is the secret to being happily married, they will mention something about *health*. If I sat next to someone who has been around a long time, he or she would always say health. If your health goes, so does everything else! If you are rich but you have poor health…there goes all your money. If you have a solid relationship, but then one person is not able to participate in the partnership in the same way because of a health condition…that relationship will be strained. Health affects everything.

Health is critical. Health is a structure. Health is a process of life. Health is a rhythm. Health is the practice of waking up consistently and having a series of things that you do to invest in you—before you invest in others. I love the cup analogy: You must fill your cup up before you pour into others. Whether it be at work, in relationships, with a spouse, with family, or with friends, if you are consistently giving of yourself without taking time to feed your mind, body, and soul, you cannot hope to be healthy. You will reach a tipping point. Eventually, you will burn out. Ultimately, you will be the worst version of yourself. You will be fat while the rest of the people around you are skinny. You will be tired while everyone else will be rested. You never want to be an unhealthy person teaching physical education. Or a poor person leading finance classes. So if you want people to see something of value in you, you must first value yourself.

The Whole Picture

To be completely and entirely H.E.R.O.I.C. in your health, you must be willing to dig into the following three areas: mind, body, and soul. Typically, these areas are most effectively developed in conjunction with one another. The smartest people will say, *"I solved that problem...while on the treadmill."* Mind, body, and soul need to be maintained throughout your lifespan. This is particularly true if you are in the military. The military says that you come second. You need to figure out a way to make yourself come first while existing in the military's system.

MIND

Read

Readers are leaders and leaders are readers. You need to read a lot. While in the military, you eat sleep and work alongside your fellow soldiers, sailors, marines, and airman. As a result, you begin to get stuck in this military mindset or lane. And while on that path, it is difficult to see what is happening outside of it. What is happening in the real world? Reading does so much to broaden our horizons and thinking.

> "NOT ALL READERS ARE LEADERS, BUT ALL LEADERS ARE READERS."
> **HARRY S. TRUMAN**

Write

Your brain is designed for processing information, not storing data. The military issues green books with a pen, so I would always carry that book in my left back pocket. I would write anything that was worth remembering. I found that I quickly adopted a test-taking mindset. I would pay special attention if a higher ranking person said phrases like "This will be on the test..." or "You will be in trouble if..." or "The mission will fail if...." When it became critical, I would write it in my book. If I needed to know it to ensure that I was successful, it went in the book.

Writing is also a method for staying connected to those you love. If it feels awkward to write "Dear Diary," one option is to write letters to those you love most. Tell them about how you are doing. Talk about your day—good and bad. Process life with your spouse, kids, parents, or friends. Whether you give them the journal is up to you. However, the process of writing it will be beneficial for your health and help you feel more connected to those you love.

Reflect

You need to be able to get away. Go hunt. Fish. Get off base. Sit in a diner and talk to strangers. Ask them about their lives and learn from others. Look at old letters or journals and assess where you have been. Think about where you want to go and about your goals. This personal time ensures that you remain centered and have the opportunity for internal and personal reflection.

Personal Reflection Questions:

1. What activities do you do to unwind?

   _____
   _____
   _____
   _____
   _____
   _____

2. What is good in your life right now?

   _____
   _____
   _____
   _____
   _____
   _____

3. What is sucking in your life right now?

   _____
   _____
   _____
   _____
   _____
   _____

4. What is your plan to move from sucking to succeeding?

   _____
   _____
   _____
   _____
   _____
   _____

Act NOW!

<u>Time Limit</u>: Five Minutes

<u>Mission</u>: Learn something new.

1. List the top five things you learned in the last five minutes.

   1. _____
   2. _____
   3. _____
   4. _____
   5. _____

Homework:

- **Read a book this week.**

BODY

Physical activity should happen in the morning because life has not happened yet. Make a point to be active between the time you wake up and the time you have your first meal. Research demonstrates that people who work out in the morning are more consistent than people who work out at any other point in the day. The morning block does not have anyone else buying for your time.

Health is the preparatory process. Think about the preparation that happens before an important interview. Or a big date. Or before you put on your swimsuit. In each of these cases, your external shell is a representation of your internal commitment.

Here is the <u>Three Ingredient Recipe</u> for physical health:

1. Meal prep and plan: I suck at this, but it just needs to happen.
2. Consistent morning workouts: Target heart rate for fifty minutes, three times/week.
3. Burn more calories than you eat. (All food is fuel, so eat accordingly. Better fuel = better performance!)

Personal Reflection Questions:

1. What are some of your fitness goals?
   _____
   _____
   _____

2. What are some things preventing you from reaching your fitness goals?
   _____
   _____

Act NOW!

Time Limit: Five Minutes

Mission: List five things you can do to live a healthier lifestyle. Do five push-ups!

1. _____
2. _____
3. _____
4. _____
5. _____

Homework:

- Pick one item on the list and do it for one week.

SOUL

For God and Country! There are so many services that the military provides to protect our First Amendment rights. As such, regardless of your religious beliefs or affiliations, the military must provide you with a way to worship in a manner that you see fit. I believe that if you serve your country, God will play a crucial role, whether you believe in it or not. There are times of incredible loneliness and sadness. There are times when you have been in a gun battle, pinned down for nine hours; you have not eaten, you are exasperated, and your emotions are on a high, and you are wondering what the point of it all is. Or you have hiked for seven miles, and your body is at the end of the rope. You will need an outlet. You need to be able to cry out to God.

The military is a lonely place. It will pull you away from your entire support system. When I was shipped to Korea, no one said, "Here are your three closest friends. Here is your buddy system." No, the military said, "We will see *you* in Korea, Shane." I was alone: at the airport, on the plane, landing, at the foreign airport. No one found me and said, "Hey, I am supposed to take you to your dorm?" I found my way on my own, and then I sat in my room alone. The military can be an isolating place. Especially if there is someone you care about who is not able to be with you.

During my time in the military, I coped with the loneliness through personal indulgences and living for myself. At the time, a fellow airman named Vince said that he wanted to invest in me. He spent months befriending me, listening to my problems and trying to support me. On multiple occasions, he gently tried to point out that I was acting like an idiot. He knew there was more to life and that I was shortchanging myself by living a life of pleasure-seeking. It reached a point where he said that he was done trying to help me until I wanted to help myself. He said I was a lost cause until I looked to something bigger. There was no reason for us to talk again. The loss of that mentor helped me reach the end of myself. I decided something had to change!

Whether you believe in God or not, at some point in your service, you will need to have a God. Everyone has that moment. Everyone reaches that point. Even if you do not believe in it, lean into it. Allow yourself to find it. God showed up for me many times during my time of service.

Personal Reflection Questions:

1. When was the last time you completely reached the end of yourself?

_____
_____
_____
_____
_____
_____
_____

2. How did you make it through that situation?

_____
_____
_____
_____
_____
_____
_____
_____
_____

EXCUSES WILL ALWAYS BE THERE FOR YOU.

OPPORTUNITY WON'T.

ANONYMOUS

Becoming H.E.R.O.I.C.

H.E.R.O.I.C.

CHAPTER FIVE:

INCENTIVE HUNTER

DRIFTING:
Not mindful about the oppertunites available

DRIVEN:
Oppertunities are squandered because of self-focus

DIRECTED:
Oppertunites are used to full measure in order to benefit others.

> **INCENTIVE** (noun)
> A thing that motivates or encourages one to do something.
> A payment or concession to stimulate greater output or investment.

There is evidence that people respond significantly to incentives. If the incentive is great enough, this may even result in irrational behavior. For example, psychologists have discovered through experimentation that when you hand a person an unexpectedly hot cup of coffee, he typically drops the cup if he perceives it to be inexpensive. However, if he believes the cup is valuable, he will manage to hang on, even if it results in a burnt hand. Incentives matter. And incentives especially matter to someone who wants to live an H.E.R.O.I.C. life.

Indeed, the response to incentives may be as innate as any other instinctive behavior. In a series of experiments at Texas A&M University, researchers have allowed rats and pigeons to "purchase" various forms of food and drink by pushing various levers. Each item has its price, such as three lever pushes for a drop of root beer or ten for a piece of cheese. The animals are given "incomes" (equal to a certain number of pushes per day). After the income is exhausted, the levers become inoperable. In some versions of the experiments, the animals can earn additional income by performing various tasks. They earn additional lever pushes at a fixed wage rate for each job they perform.

The researchers have found that rats and pigeons respond appropriately to changes in prices, changes in income, and changes in wage rates. When the price of root beer goes up, they buy less root beer. When wage rates go up, they work harder -- unless their incomes are already very high, in which case they choose to enjoy more leisure. These are precisely the responses that economists expect and observe among human beings. Fortunately, or unfortunately, incentives are only effective when they are actively pursued and effectively utilized. To live an H.E.R.O.I.C. life, it is necessary to the right perspective, motivation, mindset, and education regarding incentives.

GETTING SOME PERSPECTIVE

I bought a first-class ticket for the first time in my life. I was so excited! I had visions flying in style. It was going to be a fight of bliss: plenty of room, being waited upon, delicious food, and fabulous drinks – the works!

Well… I miss the flight! I arrived two minutes after they closed the door. I had to sit in the concourse and watch my luxury flight pull away. They were able to find me another ticket that would get me to my destination. (It consisted of a five-hour flight in coach.) I sulked onto the plane, found my *middle* seat and sat in a pool of disappointment. As I am sitting there, pissed and frustrated, I had this moment where I needed to make a choice. Was I going to let the next five hours suck? I wanted to be in first class. I felt I deserved the first class appreciation for my money. I was paying for a level of comfort that I wanted.

So I did it – I made the decision that I was going to open myself up to not making this flight suck. I looked at the lady sitting next to me, and I asked her,

"What kind of flight are you looking for? Would you like to sleep for the next few hours and ride in peace or would you like to make a new friend?"

She responded, *"I would love to meet you!"*

So I said, *"Tell me about yourself."*

I proceeded to ask her a bunch of questions about her life, interests, and goals. As we had our conversation, I kept getting free drinks delivered to me. I got a free meal. They used my name. I had no idea why but they provided me with excellent service. It was better than being in first class!

It turns out that the women I was chatting with was one of the uppity-ups in the airline. She was doing a flight hop. The more we related, the more she gave winks to the attendants and the more service I received. I was completely taken aback. I asked for her name and sent flowers to her office as a little *thank you*. This whole process was able to happen because of a conscious decision to go against my feelings of anger and choose to have a good attitude in the midst of disappointment.

This minor yet H.E.R.O.I.C. shift resulted in so many more people being encouraged (this woman, the flight attendants, our assistants) and so much more was done for the greater good than just little old me sitting in first class getting drunk on my own awesomeness.

The story did not end there. After our plane landed and I gathered my luggage I found my Uber car. I had no geographical idea how far away I was from my destination. I got into the car and told my driven where I needed to be. He typed it into the GPS and said, *"Sir that is five hours away."*
I was thinking *Five hours! What the Hell!*
He responded, *"I need to get food and gas, but I will take you!"*
So we spent the next five hours touring the Florida countryside. The entire time I was posting my adventures to Facebook.

Look here; I had the opportunity to meet a generous lady and receive first class service if I was open to it. I had the chance to explore a new, beautiful place with my Uber friend. At last, when I finally arrived at my destination, my friends, who had been following my posts, enjoyed the story so much that it became the running story for the weekend. I would have missed out on this whole incredible experience had I not made the conscious choice to have a good attitude. The world is full of adventures and incentive opportunities; however, to fulling take advantage of these, you must adopt an H.E.R.O.I.C. perspective.

FREE FRIES: IT IS ALL ABOUT RELATIONSHIPS

My wife jokes that I can get free fries at any restaurant we visit. I want to be able to walk into any dining establishment and be able to get free fries. I realize that sounds simple. And it has nothing to do with free food. It is a nod, a wink, a small gesture. However, it means that I made an impact on a life and the person responded accordingly.

I want to significantly impact others; therefore I need to have this mindset: every person matters! I need to notice the server. I want to be in genuine relationship with them, at least for that moment. So I do not shrug them off. I try to look them in the eye. If you think about it, they serve you, bless you and provide you with service. They really present you with an incredible opportunity to *serve and bless them* with a kind word or a pleasant interaction.

Living an H.E.R.O.I.C. life means that you fundamentally understand the following: if you want to be a good friend you need to be looking for ways to be friendly. If you seek an opportunity to be genuine with others, they will return the favor. It is always amazing to me how many people do not take full advantage of this concept. Most times, people keep their head down and stay in their world, only focused on themselves and what directly affects them. As a result, they are miserable, lonely, selfish and unpleasant. Whether it is due to past pain or hurt, or habit it results in a rut and vicious cycle. The H.E.R.O.I.C. approach breaks this cycle and frees you to fully invest in others and enjoy the response!

Personal Reflection Questions:

1. List 5 things that someone else did for you today?
   1. _____
   2. _____
   3. _____
   4. _____
   5. _____

2. The last time you were in a restaurant how did you treat the people that served you?
   _____
   _____
   _____
   _____
   _____

Homework:

- Challenge: Try to get free fires or a different kind of incentive due to how you responded to the people in your environment.

THE "GET TO" METHOD

Focusing on the *get to* rather than the *have to* it will change your whole perspective and lead to an H.E.R.O.I.C. and fulfilling life. I *get to* breathe fresh air. I *get to* walk or run. I *get to* have food in my belly. I *get to* earn money for defending freedom.

It is so easy to see the things you have taken for granted when they are taken away. I take for granted food until I am hungry and there is nothing to eat. I take for granted my phone until it falls in the toilet. I take for granted my spouse until they die or leave me.

What if you were able to alter your thinking so that you genuinely saw the positive things in your life as *gifts* rather than *givens*? How much would your day, week, month, and life change if you looked at each gift and said *thank you* through your attitude, responses, or relationships? Now instead of pissing and moaning, it presents an opportunity for gratitude and optimism. Below are examples of problems that can ruin your day. However, if you choose to have an H.E.R.O.I.C. mindset, any situation can turn to the positive.

For example:

- *I scraped my knee → I am thankful that I usually do not have knee problems*
- *I have to work today → I am grateful. I know that there are people who that cannot find a job.*
- *My wife left me → I can start anew with someone who wants to be with me*
- *I had a shitty childhood → My horrible upbringing impacted who I am until this point, but it will not define my current relationships or future direction.*

A gracious and thankful attitude it shines on everything you do. It becomes the mark of an H.E.R.O.I.C. life. Everything turns into a ***get to***!

- I *get to* serve those people that are safe at home.
- I *get to* go to training.
- I *get to* study and learn.
- I *get to* work extra hours and develop my skills and relationships.
- I *get to* meet new people at that new duty station.

Personal Reflection Questions:

1. List 5 task that you do not like to do but are required to do?

   1. _____

   2. _____

   3. _____

   4. _____

   5. _____

2. How can the list above be turned to opportunities to benefit you or others?

   1. _____

   2. _____

   3. _____

   4. _____

   5. _____

SOME INCENTIVES FOR MILITARY PERSONNEL

- **Housing Funds** – Remember, do not Over-Adult too soon. In the case of the military, they provide for housing and food. You can literally "not adult" for a while. Typically young adults enlist and try to catch up to their parents in the course of a year.

- **School and Education** – In those down times, when you have nothing to do, might as well learn. You can take tests and go to college. The military has embraced education. There is a University of Maryland *Asia*! The University of Phoenix is huge – all you need is the internet! Almost every prominent college campus now has a military version.

- **Sick Call Warrior** – There is this mindset that it is not American or some lacks integrity if they go to the doctor. It is not part of the brotherhood to give into sickness. We are trained to suck it up and deal. Because when you go to the doctor, someone else has to cover your job. Now I am not talking to the people that know how to abuse the system to get out of work – they do exist and you know who you are. However, the military provides so many services to ensure that you stay healthy and well. Take advantage of all the medical and dental services provided. They want to fix anything that is broken or hurting. The military took care of all of my dental work – now I smile all the time!

- **Enlistment Bonuses:** Some bonuses require enlisting for longer than the standard four-year enlistment. Enlistment bonuses are continually changing depending on recruiting needs. Make sure to ask your recruiter for details.

- **Student Loan Repayment:** If you have gone to college or are going to school, and have loans to repay, the military may be able to help.

- **Voluntary Education Programs:** Many military members continue their education while on active duty. Each of the services has programs dedicated to helping their members reach their education goals. These programs offer tuition assistance, counseling, classroom facilities, and other systems to support voluntary education.

- **G.I. Bill:** In a nutshell, the G.I. Bill gives educational benefits. Although you may begin using this incentive while you are on active duty, you must earn an honorable discharge if you choose to use your benefits after service.

- **Accelerated Promotion**: Accelerated promotion is offered through several methods. You may be eligible if you:

    - Were/are a Girl or Boy Scout.
    - Have college credit or have already earned a college degree.
    - Refer friends to join.
    - Were a member of the Civil Air Patrol
    - Participated in Junior Reserve Officer Training (JROTC) in high school

- **Special Forces Recruitment:** The Army, Navy, and Air Force offer special incentives for recruits who sign up for special forces programs. These programs are extremely competitive, and you should only consider the Special Forces if you are in great physical and mental shape. Visit the Special Operations Center to see if you have what it takes.

ENTHUSIASM IS THE MOTHER OF EFFORT, AND WITHOUT IT NOTHING GREAT WAS EVER ACHIEVED.

– RALPH WALDO EMERSON

Becoming H.E.R.O.I.C.

H.E.R.O.I.C.

CHAPTER SIX:
COURAGE AND COMMITMENT

DRIFTING:
Ruled by fear and lack of motivation.

DRIVEN:
Motivated by selfish desires and wishes.

DIRECTED:
Deep resolve to help others.

COURAGE

Courage is an attribute of every hero. It is the choice and the willingness to confront agony, pain, danger, uncertainty or intimidation. *Physical* courage is bravery in the face of physical pain, hardship, death or threat of death. *Moral* courage is the ability to act rightly in the face of widespread opposition, shame, scandal, discouragement, or personal loss. To live an H.E.R.O.I.C. life, it is imperative to have both. According to phycologist, there are six attributes of courage. The following is an examination of these characteristics through the Heroic filter:

1. **Feeling fear yet choosing to act** – Many times fear prevents action. The feel of failure, rejection, or the unknown. The H.E.R.O.I.C. model is not designed to make fear disappear. Instead, this system has a robust and proven method that requires courage, sacrifice, and character. You are not alone in your fear or this process. Take the plunge with full commitment. It might be scary, but it is worth it! Countless lives have been improved because of this system. You have a group of fellow heroes that are working these step right alongside you!

2. **Following your heart** – Deep down everyone wants to be the best version of themselves. Typically that desire gets buried by hurt, pain, selfishness or anger. Reach down deep and find that desire to improve yourself and your situation. The desire to live an H.E.R.O.I.C. life is in all of us. Find it, follow through and watch it flourish!

3. **Persevering in the face of adversity** – There are so many times during this process that it will be easier to quit than stay the course. RESIST THE TEMPTATION TO GIVE UP! Fight. You are the hero of your story, and you can do it! Fight like your life depends on it…it actually does!

4. **Standing up for what is right** – There is great freedom in living a life of good decisions. You are in your life for the long haul. Therefore you should have a long-game mindset! The ability to make good and right decisions will benefit you today and in the future. Not only will proper choices help you *live a better life*, but you will *like yourself more* the longer you make good decisions.

5. **Expanding your horizons; letting go of the familiar** – The heroic system is designed to push you out of your comfort zone. If you truly embrace this system, you will be stretched and grow in ways you cannot imagine. There is a big world out there. You get to be an H.E.R.O.I.C. explorer of new horizons and experiences. The result will be a better you!

6. **Facing suffering with dignity or faith** – Laying down your life for others is not easy. It requires daily sacrifice. It is hard. It requires grit. It demands a level of stubborn resolve that says "I will choose to lean into difficult situations regardless of the cost because I know that the reward will be worth it!" Use that true grit and determination to improve your life and the lives of those around you. Remember to kick ass with grace and kindness!

To live an H.E.R.O.I.C. life, it is imperative to face life with courage. There will be outside pressures that will try to discourage you from living into your potential. Remember: you have the power and bravery to withstand these obstacles and rise victorious.

COMMITMENT: YOUR WORD

Honoring your commitment – are you a person of integrity and dependability? If you say that you are going to do something, will you? <u>Trust is a series of small kept promises.</u>

As previously mentioned, I decided to quit drinking. Not drinking is a daily decision and commitment. People look at me and think that I have it all together. I do not. No one does. It requires making a choice every day. *Today* am I going to live into the promises I made for myself yesterday. Over time the hill does not disappear, but it does get easier to climb.

The exciting thing is that being different, unique and having courage and convictions in life inspires others and draws attention! For example, recently I was invited to the Wisconsin for a trip they called MANCA. (Man + Vacation = Mancation, shortened to MANCA.) There were six of us attending. I only knew one other person before arriving. I had no idea what the weekend would hold, but I felt strangely out of my comfort zone because of the dialogue that was happening before our trip. Most of the conversations were centered around drinking. I questioned if I would be able to find commonalities with these men.

When we arrived, the pace of the trip was slow, and the conversations were deep. Each guy had a different backstory. Some had tough childhoods; others had fond memories of summer family vacations. Some men were popular, some had been bullied, and some had been loners. We shared our various perspectives on a range of topics: work ethic, dedication to family, marriage, convictions and personal and professional mishaps.

I found myself interested in every story. It dawned on me; our stories are all connected. Each of us walks a unique path, but no one walks the path alone. We are meant to learn from one another and grow side by side. The weekend was not about drinking at all; it was about connecting.

This is what the H.E.R.O.I.C. model is all about: connecting with yourself and others in a meaningful and positive ways. The cool thing is that three of the men there saw that I was having just as much fun without alcohol and they made a commitment to give up drinking for one year just to see if made a difference in their lives. By keeping a promise to myself, others were inspired to be a better version of themselves! That is the purpose of this H.E.R.O.I.C. system: bring people together and make their lives better – individually and collectively!

Personal Reflection Questions:

1. Do you honor your commitments? Would others say that you are a person of your word?

2. What prevents you from honoring your commitments? What keeps you accountable to fulfilling your obligations?

PUSH ON

Throughout life, there are always going to be people and circumstances that will try to knock you off your feet. It is so easy in our society to get drawn into the darker, more depressing details of life. The best way to combat this and stay positive is to follow these practical tips. Do not let the negativity get to you. Be H.E.R.O.I.C. and to try to overcome it in the most positive ways possible. Keep your home and workplace simple, encouraging, and proactive

1. **Try not to take it personally** – If you are dealing with someone who has a "toxic" personality, just remember this: it's none of your business what any other person thinks of you, and it does not affect you. If they think negatively of you, who cares? Just be you and be the bigger person.

2. **Keep your cool** – By not lowering yourself to the standards of negative people, you will find it is much easier to stay calm, stay positive, and just accept the state of things as they are until you can get out.

3. **Remove yourself from the situation** – It may seem like an easy out, but it is

sometimes the best choice. If you cannot get out, sometimes backing out of a negative conversation and daydreaming for a minute is enough to keep the negativity from sticking to you.

4. **Breathe** – Any good therapist will recommend breathing therapy to ease anxiety, and it works. The next step (Step 5) is a great way to follow it up.

5. **Count to 10. If that doesn't work, count to 20** – Works like a charm. It gives you a few seconds to let go of your instinctive reaction so that you do not let the negativity affect you.

6. **Exercise** – Even if you are only exercising for 15 minutes a few times a week, you will feel better, and your head will be clear.

7. **Speak up** – If you are ready and willing, fight the negativity with your (positive) words. Just be prepared to defend your position, and keep a steady head, or else you will end up lowering your standards without realizing it.

8. **Keep yourself occupied** – If your mind is focused on something else, it is easier to ignore the pessimism surrounding you.

9. **Surround yourself with things that help you stay positive** – surround yourself with things that make you content and keep you uplifted. It doesn't matter if it's sticky notes with optimistic quotes, photos of family, or listening to music that brings you back to a positive place.

10. **Don't hold grudges** – It's just not good for you. It is like drinking poison and expecting the other person to die! It will bring you down to a self-destructive place, and it can be very hard to transport yourself away from there, the longer time goes on. Remember, forgiveness is not about the other person. Forgiveness is for you. It is about moving forward and letting go.

11. **Make your home your retreat** – Since negativity can be overwhelming in today's world, the most stable place to boost positivity is in your home. You owe it to yourself to turn your home into a peaceful oasis, where you can come home and leave the negativity at the door.

Personal Reflection Questions:

1. What strategies from the list above can you implement to combat negativity?

   _____
   _____
   _____
   _____
   _____

2. Are there individuals in your life that cause you to feel negative and sad?

   _____
   _____
   _____
   _____
   _____

3. Are there individuals in your life that inspire you to be the best person you can be?

   _____
   _____
   _____
   _____
   _____

Act NOW!

<u>Time Limit</u>: 5 Minutes

<u>Mission</u>: List five things you can do to live a healthier lifestyle.

Homework:

- Challenge: Try to get free fires or a different kind of incentive because of how you responded to the people in your environment.

Get Connected:

- Post a picture or message about the last incentive you got! #HEROICrewards

LEAVING A LEGACY

The lessons of faithful service and sacrifice are never-ending. It is still a personal struggle today. I still want my name first. I want to be the best. I want to give money in secret but then whisper to everyone, did you see what I did? I want approval from people. However, if I am going to leave a legacy that is greater than me, I need to make it about others and not myself.

There is an element of life that what you do unto others will become an abundance in your own life. The more that you give to others, the more they will want to give to you. Furthermore, they will want to invest in you and your success. If you decided to spend your time investing in the lives of others, you would ultimately be wealthier, more wise, more connected and more loved! Therefore you must make this H.E.R.O.I.C. journey about improving yourself and also about improving the lives of others. For instance, you should consider how each step of the H.E.R.O.I.C. process benefits you and those around you!

Have Purpose
- You: What are you living for?
- Others: How will it affect others?

Entrepreneur Mindset

- You: Is your money working for you or against you?
- Others: How is your money being used to bless others?

Relationship

- You: What are you doing to be the best version of yourself?
- Others: Are you investing in others or using them for personal gain?

Overall Health

- You: Are your body, mind, and soul effective at accomplishing your goals?
- Others: How can you care for others without caring for yourself?

Incentive Hunter

- You: Part of giving heroically is receiving gracefully. Do you take full advantage of all the gifts being given to you?
- Others: How can I use those gifts for others? Who is coming with me?

Courage and Commitment

- You: Do you have the pure tenacity and grit required to accomplish your objectives?
- Others: What type of legacy are you leaving for others?

BECOMING
H.E.R.O.I.C.
A FINAL NOTE

BECOMING H.E.R.O.I.C.

If you live an intentional life, full of love and resolve, and you reflect on yourself and your progress every day (perhaps every moment), you will inevitably become the best version of yourself. It is imperative that you take the necessary time to honestly reflect on yourself, establish goals and develop a plan of execution.

The H.E.R.O.I.C. model provides six clear areas of consideration and evaluation. By following this Success Playbook, it is possible to ensure that you are thriving in any circumstance life throws your way. This process is completely effective, but ultimately your success comes down to you. Do you have the ware withal and correct mindset to move from Drifting to Driven to Directed in all areas of your life?

The H.E.R.O.I.C. process is like building the foundation of a house. Each component is meant to be strong independently. You need to have a plan, good materials, and correct support. That is what the H.E.R.O.I.C. model provides for you. However, it does not stop there. You can have a pile of beautiful elements that will never turn into a wall until you put in the work!

The alarm clock rings. It is 04:00. The bed is warm and sleep feels SO good. What makes the difference between pushing the snooze button three more times and stepping into the cold air to go for your morning run? Too many people are pushing the Snooze button on their own life! No Olympic gold medalist has ever stood on that podium and said: "Man I am sure glad I slept in all those months." No elite athlete has ever danced in the sprinkle of confetti as a champion and said: "This is for the hours of binge-watching Netflix!" And certainly, no couple celebrating their 60th Wedding Anniversary has said, "I am sure glad I started neglecting my spouse 30 years ago". There is no shortcut to anything worth doing! And yet, it is so easy to just give into laziness and selfishness. It is almost as though we humans are programmed to do that! Be H.E.R.O.I.C. and fight that innate urge!

All of life occurs in seasons. There are sometimes when one area of your life is going great, but your relationships are struggling. Or maybe your relationships are awesome, and you are dealing with health issues. The key to the H.E.R.O.I.C. Model is that we are all in process. We all have strengths to celebrate and weaknesses to conquer. Real heroes do not shy away from the difficulties of life. We reach into the deepest part of our resolve, and then we reach farther! Sheer grit and determination push us onward. As you continue to develop your H.E.R.O.I.C. skills, remember the importance of life-long assessment. Become best friends with input and evaluation. Read this book as often as you are struggling. Implement the lessons and checkpoints that address your current areas of struggle. Remember to continue to reach out to other members of our H.E.R.O.I.C. community. The responsibility to live an H.E.R.O.I.C. life is in your power, but we do have a powerful team that wants to support you! The rest of us are in the fight of our lives. We are warriors defending our families. We are fighters attacking each moment to ensure we use it to our full advantage. We are H.E.R.O.I.C. in business, fitness, relationships, and life. Join us if you have a deep desire and unwavering courage to be significant! We look forward to seeing you on the battlefield!

BECOMING

H.E.R.O.I.C.

RESOURCES

ABOUT SHANE MCGRAW

As a U.S Military veteran, Shane McGraw understands the sacrifice veterans and their families make for our country. That is why he is dedicated his career to serving veterans just like you! Shane and his team will help you understand and navigate what will likely be one of the most significant purchases of your life. Furthermore, Shane McGraw understands firsthand the importance and stability that home ownership brings to all members of the military.

Shane began his career in mortgage lending in 2006 after leaving the military. Since then, he has closed more than 2,000 home loans. He believes that the home financing process required a firm plan that accounts for the short- and long-term goals of each buyer, and that is precisely what you will receive when you work with Shane and his team.

Shane is a husband, father, and an avid Seahawks fan. He is also an active member of his church and the local community. Shane enjoys coaching, mentoring, and walking alongside other men as they chase after their H.E.R.O.I.C. story.

ABOUT THE SHANE MCGRAW TEAM

The Shane McGraw Team strives to create Loving Profitable Relationships by not only meeting but exceeding expectations. We deliver world-class service demonstrated through honesty, hard work, and responsibility. In doing so, we all win! Our clients receive exceptional service, our business partners make more money, and we maintain a healthy business. The relationship is far more important than any transaction.

Whatever your situation may be, The Shane McGraw Team will help you understand the options available to you and guide you through each step of the home financing process — all while giving you the honesty and respect you deserve.

Our team is ready to help you identify and obtain the right home loan or refinancing solution for your situation. We will answer any questions you may have, keep you informed throughout the process and get your loan closed as quickly as possible. Simply complete a loan application from the options available, and we will contact you.

Therefore if you are looking for home financing, contact our team today to learn more and get pre-qualified!

Please Call: 360.519.7567

2819 NW Kitsap Pl, Ste. 204 Silverdale, Washington

BOOK SHANE MCGRAW TO SPEAK AT YOUR NEXT EVENT!

ShaneMcGrawTeam.com
mcgrawteam@myccmortgage.com
http://www.shanemcgrawteam.com
360.519.7567

Made in the USA
Columbia, SC
27 November 2017